Ending *the* Search for
Mr. Right

michelle mckinney hammond

HARVEST HOUSE PUBLISHERS

EUGENE, OREGON

Unless otherwise indicated, all Scripture quotations are taken from the HOLY BIBLE, NEW INTER-NATIONAL VERSION®. NIV®. Copyright © 1973, 1978, 1984 by the International Bible Society. Used by permission of Zondervan. All rights reserved.

Verses marked NKJV are taken from the New King James Version. Copyright © 1982 by Thomas Nelson, Inc. Used by permission. All rights reserved.

Verses marked NASB are taken from the New American Standard Bible®, © 1960, 1962, 1963, 1968, 1971, 1972, 1973, 1975, 1977, 1995 by The Lockman Foundation. Used by permission. (www.Lockman.org)

Verses marked NLT are taken from the *Holy Bible*, New Living Translation, copyright © 1996. Used by permission of Tyndale House Publishers, Inc., Wheaton, IL 60189. All rights reserved.

Verses marked KJV are taken from the King James Version of the Bible.

Cover by Koechel Peterson & Associates, Minneapolis, Minnesota

Published in association with the literary agency of Alive Communications, Inc., 7680 Goddard Street, Suite 200, Colorado Springs, CO 80920.

ENDING THE SEARCH FOR MR. RIGHT

Copyright © 2005 by Michelle McKinney Hammond
Published by Harvest House Publishers
Eugene, Oregon 97402
www.harvesthousepublishers.com

Library of Congress Cataloging-in-Publication Data

McKinney Hammond, Michelle, 1957–
    Ending the search for Mr. Right / Michelle McKinney Hammond.
        p. cm.
    ISBN 0-7369-1505-2 (pbk.)
    1. Single women—Religious life. 2. Mate selection—Religious aspects—Christianity.
3. Bible. O.T. Ruth—Criticism, interpretation, etc. I. Title.
BV4596.S5M344 2005
241'.6765—dc22   2004015769

Printed in the United States of America

05   06   07   08   09   10   11   / VP-KB /   10   9   8   7   6   5   4   3   2   1

Contents

Attention, Please...

*L*adies, it is time to get down to the nitty-gritty on this finding-a-man thing. And why not? It is on everybody's minds, for the most part. The time has come to get matters of the heart in perspective and lay some sound ground rules for finding and keeping love in our lives. I know it can be troubling when we take a look around us. We are tempted to say, "Where are all the men?" Well, they are out there. And they are wondering the same thing about us! This might seem impossible, and yet it is true. For men and women alike, finding "The One" seems to be as elusive as finding a needle in a haystack. Could we possibly be contributing to this problem? This is what I would like to address in my time with you.

Several evenings ago, before leaving for a road trip, a friend and I decided to grab a quick dinner at a restaurant that had just opened in my neighborhood. This restaurant had quickly become the new "she-she-pooh-pooh-la-la" place. That means the "in" spot for all the beautiful, upwardly mobile people—the yuppies, buppies, and other uppies. Though it was early, we were told that the dining room was full. If we liked, we could be seated in the lounge and order from the menu there. We were then escorted to the lower level of the restaurant and greeted by pulsating music and a dreamlike atmosphere. Couples, female clusters, male partners, and mixed groups of friends were lounging and reclining, languidly gazing around the room, or caught up in animated conversation.

I was starving when I entered the room, but my hunger was quickly forgotten as I took in the scene before me. Call me a workaholic, but I was amazed that this was what people do in the middle of the week. First of all, I was struck by the fact that it was a Thursday night, a work night, and these people had obviously gone home, showered, and changed just to come out to see and be seen. The men were looking, the women were strutting, but no one was connecting. To be perfectly honest, I felt a bit naive. I had left this sort of scene so long ago that the subtleties of it were no longer clear to me. I had vague remembrances of my B.C. days (before establishing a relationship with Christ) of hanging out, meeting guys at the bar or on the dance floor, and having brief flings that never went anywhere. After all, how seriously could you take someone you had met under these circumstances?

There always seemed to be a cloud of suspicion hanging over these newfound dates. Where had they come from? Were they seeing anyone else? Who were their friends? What was their background? Who were they really? Were they always on the prowl? Had fate actually worked in your favor on that chance encounter? Too many questions and uncertainties usually clouded any potential for true love with trust issues before two people could even get started. That night, it seemed that nothing had changed except that men were much bolder years ago. They clocked the woman they wanted and moved in for the kill, because everyone understood that was what we were all out for. This new scene of people passing one another in a solo dance that was designed for two was troubling at best.

"What was the point?" my friend and I asked. Here were all these women dressed to the nines, I mean *really* dressed to impress: backless, strapless, short short, spike heels, flawless makeup...and not a bite. They got lots of stares, but no takers.

I wondered, as we left, if anyone made a love connection before the evening was over, and how many people went home disappointed that once again their search for love had turned up empty. How many men kicked themselves for not saying "hello"? How many women wondered if they should have gone up and introduced themselves or been more aggressive or worn a different outfit?

How ironic that in a world where everyone longs for the same thing, true love remains elusive for many. If everyone is searching for love, why is it so hard for us to find one another? That mystery question will be answered when someone finally figures out why traffic is backed up if all the cars are moving on a highway. It is one of the great mysteries of life.

Can the search for love be fruitful? I believe it can be when we plant the right seeds and purposefully apply ourselves to living lives that invite love to find us. Because love is not just a feeling but a decision, the head must work with the heart to make intelligent choices that lead to love. As we take a look at an ancient account of a young woman who found lasting love in the most unexpected place, we will dissect the story of Ruth and Boaz—found in the book of Ruth in the Bible—to find principles that can be applied to our own lives. But first, I must ask you some questions:

- ✩ Are you really ready for the love you think you want?

- ✩ What is your motivation for desiring a committed love relationship?

- ✩ What problems do you think love will solve in your world?

- ✩ What are you prepared to give in order to get the love you desire?

✫ Are you willing to make changes in your world to accommodate the man you love?

✫ Do you know what you want in a man?

✫ Do you know what you *should* want in a man?

✫ Are your expectations of love realistic?

✫ If you never found Mr. Right, would you still be able to lead a happy and fulfilled life?

These questions might take some time and deep thought for you to answer, but certain heart issues must be settled before we even begin. Though we do not often think about men as being intuitive, they do indeed possess this trait when it comes to women. They can sense desperation, unresolved issues, and excess emotional baggage from a mile away. Believe me, once they get a whiff of any of these, they head for the hills.

This book is less about men and more about you, although I will tell you what you need to look for in a man and what the appropriate responses should be once he finds you. Notice I said *he* finds *you*. It is the job of a *real* man to find his woman, pursue her, and capture her heart. It is the job of the woman to be ready to be found—a much easier job description. But it will only be easy if you have your head and your heart together.

So let's begin. I suggest you grab a journal and chronicle your feelings and gut reactions as you read. It is time to settle your issues and prepare yourself to be loved and to love in return.

1

Love Hunger

In the days when the judges ruled,
there was a famine in the land...

RUTH 1:1

So begins the story of hunger, longing, unfulfillment, and even starvation. I am actually fascinated when I meet a woman who has an active dating life. As I travel the country speaking to and greeting women, the number of those who have not had a date in years is staggering. The common complaint is that all the good men are taken, in jail, or gay. Many women have decided to steer their passions in other directions—toward their careers or other self-fulfilling habits like shopping or being involved in social or charitable activities. Yet in each woman's heart the hunger remains to be loved by that one man who will come into her life, sweep her off her feet, and rock her world.

Turn on your television any day of the week and it is clearly evident that when it comes to the search for love, we are in a state of emergency. The plethora of matchmaking stunts reveals the urgency of men and women, no matter what race or class, to try to find true love at all costs. Some people are even willing to embarrass themselves on a national scale to compete for the attention of a bachelor or bachelorette. The looks of disappointment and the level of frustration displayed after not being chosen *by a stranger* tell the tale. People are desperate. Men and women feel their options for finding a lasting, committed relationship are quickly vanishing, along with their hopes to fulfill their deepest longing: to love and be loved.

The hunger for love can do strange things to a woman. It can cause her to question herself and her worth. She can plummet to new depths of insecurity and despair, getting caught up in late-night eating binges, compulsive self-consumption, bitterness, frustration, paralysis, and letting herself go physically. Putting life on hold until the knight arrives only heightens her aggravation because she is now not only *alone*, but also bored. This leads her on a more frenzied search for something that will put out the fire of yearning that nestles deep within the soul.

Her search for love swings the gamut from endless conversations with other friends in the same situation to unproductive seasons of self-involvement that include self-defeating, unhealthy habits. Many a meal is eaten while pondering the resounding question, "Where have all the good men gone?" As the answer appears more and more elusive, resolutions are drawn that life can go on without the special man. Yet hunger ignored simply burrows deeper into the inner recesses of the heart and manifests itself in other ways. The problem with hunger is that it is real. How we feed it has an effect on our health—physically, emotionally, and spiritually.

When we are hungry physically, and we are not in the position to have a balanced, healthy meal, we have a tendency to settle for junk food. We choose empty calories or something that is filling but also fattening, seemingly satisfying but not nutritious. When we are hungry emotionally, we can make choices that are just as unhealthy. We settle for what is available: no-win relationships with men that we know are not good for us, who could never be prospects for a committed relationship. This is when we discover that empty relationships can be more harmful than empty calories. Many times we emerge from these relationships with more baggage, more disabling deadweight, and an even deeper hunger from all the negative experiences we endured for the sake of having an "affirming moment" here and there.

No one should crucify herself for wanting love. The longing for love is a natural human emotion. It is a spiritual instinct, built into the center of our souls by the Author of love Himself: God. God also longs for love from all of His creation. He placed this hunger inside us to cause us to reach first for Him, and secondly for one another. We should desire to love and be loved. But the desire for love should not rule us to the point where we look for it in all the wrong places, trying to fulfill our longing with unhealthy alternatives, or becoming paralyzed by our yearning.

I have always warned people that it is not a good idea to go grocery shopping when you are hungry. When our eyes are bigger than our stomachs, we have a tendency to make bad choices and end up with things that we do not need. Everything looks good when we are hungry. We will pay a high price for hunger that is out of control. At the end of the day, we still will not be satisfied. Those women who have settled for *something* rather than having *nothing* in the area of relationships have found themselves more miserable than when they were alone.

How did our hunger become so overwhelming if it is a God-given instinct? We might say that from the moment our mother Eve and her husband, Adam, shared a bite out of the forbidden fruit in the garden, women the world over inherited the consequences of her little afternoon snack. The punishment for deciding that God was not enough to fulfill all of her desires landed her in a place where her appetite would never be satisfied. Validation and affirmation from her husband, Mr. Adam,

Man Fact:
A man can never totally satisfy your craving for love. His humanity will not allow him to.

would never hit the spot in her heart where she wanted it to. Eve would always need more from him than he could give. This desire would rule over her, consume her, and become an overwhelming hunger unable to be satisfied until she realized that God was the only One who could fill it.

You see, God had reserved a spot in Eve's heart for Himself. He would never allow a man to fill the spot He created for Himself because then there would be no need for Him. And He will never allow that. According to His original design, once He was allowed to sit on the throne of her heart, she would find all of her deepest desires fulfilled by Him. The man would just be the icing on the cake of her life. Her security and all that she needed would be fulfilled by the One who had created her and loved her most. However, she canceled His reservation when she decided to become "independent," to "make her own choices," and to allow something else to become more important than her connection to Him. But once she made her own choice and launched out into the deep of her own desires, she found herself hungrier than ever. I believe we inherited her hunger.

So how do we handle relationship hunger in a healthy manner? Many women have asked, "If God isn't going to give me the desire of my heart, why won't He take the desire away?" Let me help you out here. He is not going to take away your desire. He gave you that desire. You are to *have* desires; however, you are not to allow your desires to have you. He will help you to master your desires if you allow Him to.

"Well, how do I do that, Michelle?" you ask. First of all, deal with the reality of your hunger. The interesting thing about hunger is even though we may feel hunger, the body does not go into starvation mode immediately. The body is able to feed on itself for 40 days before it begins to react negatively to not having food. The first reality about love hunger is you will not die without a man in your life. Can you exist and actually thrive instead of just survive? The answer is absolutely yes! I am a witness.

Your hunger is not bad unless it is controlling you—overtaking your every thought and coloring your decisions. If this is the case, it is time to take back control. First step, get a love life. "Exactly how do I do that?" you ask. "After all, that is why I bought the book." True, so let's take it one step at a time. I am going to break this down into something you can use. If you are willing to do the work, I promise you that the truth will equip you to make yourself free. Along the way, you will find confessions in call-out boxes. I suggest you hide these confessions in your heart and let them roll around in your head until they become a part of you.

First, feed on the sources of love that God has already placed in your life. That would include God first, then you (yes, you!), and thirdly your neighbors: friends, family, and even other men. Yes, this truly can be accomplished. In order to make wise selections that are nutritious to your body, as well as your heart and soul, you must be full and whole already. The full soul will loathe even

> ## Personal Confession:
>
> *I will no longer allow my hunger to drive me into the arms of those who are undiscerning of my worth and undeserving of my heart.*

the honeycomb, but the empty soul will find even a bitter thing sweet. Remember the opening verse to this chapter? It said that when the judges ruled, there was a famine. When your flesh or emotions rule, you become a prime candidate for a famine of the heart. But when God rules, your heart is fertile ground for joyous fulfillment, regardless of if there is a man in your life or not.

Your relationship with God sets the stage for how all of your relationships will play out. Remember that the first famous commandment (not suggestion) from our heavenly Creator is: "Love the Lord your God with all your heart, soul, mind, and strength." This is followed by the second commandment that everyone knows, even if the person has never cracked open a Bible: "Love your neighbor as yourself." You cannot love anyone else properly until you love yourself, and you cannot love yourself properly unless you love God and have a passionate, intimate relationship with Him.

The One who made you loves you most. He will tell you many wonderful things about yourself, as well as His plans for you, that should have you beaming and feeling pretty good about who you are. After all, if you listen to Him long enough, you will come to believe you are pretty special, which indeed you are. However, if you are not connected intimately to the Source of love, the voices of people who dispute how fabulous you are become louder and drown out His still, small voice that whispers such great reassurances of your worth. As someone once said, "What you continually hear is what you will believe."

Once we have accepted the lie that we are not special, lovable, or desirable, we only have limited recourses in recovering any small ounce of self-worth—like putting down other people. Making them look bad will surely make us look better, or so we think. Unfortunately, that is just not true. We usually end up feeling worse than ever. Even if we are able to veil our inner loathing and control our criticisms of other people, we can fall prey to the spirit of rejection. Driven by our own lack of self-esteem, we sabotage relationship after relationship, while constantly justifying these failed relationships with our own self-debasement.

Ah…but when we are connected to the original Lover of our souls, we are brimming over with validation and affirmation that liberates us to celebrate people and even encourage them to higher heights of won-

Man Fact:
Men desire love just as much as we do, but most of them cannot handle complicated women burdened down with lots of baggage.

derfulness. In Matthew 4:4, Jesus states, "Man does not live on bread alone, but on every word that comes from the mouth of God." Notice He did not mention other relationships as a means of sustenance. After all, Adam survived and even thrived while walking and talking with God all by himself before Eve was presented to him. He did not even realize he had a need until God brought it up! If this is the case, it stands to reason that we get sustenance from God not only by reading the Bible, but also by our personal interaction with Him through prayer and fellowship. It is during the time we spend time with Him, not just talking but also listening, that life-giving words are spoken into our spirit that strengthen, renew, and fill us to overflowing with the assurance of God's faithfulness and goodness. Not only does He give us assurance of His love for us, but He also gives us the keys to living the life we want to lead.

Now that God has our ear, He promises to provide us with a great filler loaded with nutrition for our soul. He will reveal our purpose and how to operate in it. Jesus said that His nourishment came from doing the will of His Father and finishing the work He had been sent to do. How much more fulfilled do we feel when we lay our heads down at night knowing we have done what we were created to do? We have blessed someone during the day with a word, an action, or simply by just being there.

We made a difference, a lasting impression out of the bounty of our natural gifting, as we extended ourselves to someone who had a need that we could fill.

Our gifts and talents are the things people celebrate about us, but we find to be no big deal. Because the ability comes naturally to us, that is why it is called a gift. Everyone cannot do what we do the way we do it. An effectual prayer would be to ask God how to take our natural talents and

Personal Confession:

I will allow God to do the work that needs to be done in my heart to make me a whole person before I pursue a love relationship.

abilities and capitalize on them to bless people and prosper ourselves emotionally, spiritually, and perhaps even financially. That overlooked ability we have with children, decorating a room, working with numbers, planning events, or whatever—we need to use it for the benefit of other people and the glory of God. Then we can stand back and survey our handiwork and smile because someone benefited from an encounter with us.

With the Source of our fulfillment securely in place, we are then free to have and experience a myriad of relationships that can only enrich our lives. This sense of fulfillment becomes the foundation for satisfying exchanges with family members, fruitful experiences with friends, and rich platonic relationships with the men in our lives until Mr. Right comes along.

That's right, ladies. Every man you meet does not have to be "The One." Just because he is not Mr. Right does not mean you cannot have an incredible friendship. There is a lot to learn about men, and who better to learn from than a friend who will answer you honestly and live with transparency before you? The only way this can be achieved is if you are so full of love and life already that you can take or leave the appetizers that are presented to you and patiently wait for the main entrée.

Ponder This

- Are you love hungry?

- How does your hunger manifest itself? What have been the consequences?

- What parts of your life have you put on hold while waiting for a man?

- What opportunities have you not taken advantage of?

- What actions can you take right now to lead a more fulfilling life?

Why spend money on what is not bread,
and your labor on what does not satisfy? Listen,
listen to me, and eat what is good, and your soul will
delight in the richest of fare (Isaiah 55:2).

2
The Land of Do-It-Yourself

*And a certain man of Bethlehem, Judah, went to dwell
in the country of Moab...and remained there....
Then Elimelech, Naomi's husband, died.*

RUTH 1:1-3 NKJV

*W*henever we allow our love hunger to rule over us, we
begin to look for love in all the wrong places. Love hunger is not
relegated just to singles. The story tells us that a married couple,
as well as two single young men, left the safe haven of Bethlehem (which means "house of bread") in Judah (which means
"praise"), and went to a place called Moab. You see, if we do not
know our purpose, why we are where we are, we will become
distracted by our hunger, fail to realize that all we need is already
right where we are, and we will move from the place where God
has placed us in order to receive our heart's desire.

The man leading this expedition from the house of bread
was Elimelech, which means "God is my king." Amazingly,
when we are overwhelmed by hunger, we forget who we are, who
God is, and how He is able to supply all of our needs. We step
out of character and do things that go against the grain of who

we were created to be: women who trust God and His timing for their lives. Judah may be a physical place, but praise is a state of the mind and heart. Nurturing a thankful spirit in spite of what we hunger for will feed our soul faster than allowing discontent to ravage us. Discontent will always lead us astray, straight into the Land of Do-It-Yourself. That is exactly what Moab (meaning "child of her father") represents. Doing it yourself is exactly where the enemy of your soul, the enemy of your joy and peace, wants you. When you choose to do things yourself, you will always end up with more than you bargained for, which adds up to nothing good.

Let's consider how Moab came to be. After Lot fled from Sodom and Gomorrah with his two daughters, they stopped to lodge in the side of a mountain. As the two daughters considered their fate and what it meant for the future, the alarm on their biological clocks sounded. The two sisters fretted because they now had no husbands and were in danger of not being able to have children. They concocted a scheme to get their father drunk and sleep with him in order to become impregnated. The two sons they bore were named Ammon and Moab. The two sons grew into nations that were terrible enemies of Israel. Because of these nations' incestuous beginning, they inherited a nature that was distasteful to God: worshiping idols, having orgies, indulging in lascivious behavior…you name it.

Moab went a step further. The king of Moab hired the prophet Balaam to curse the nation of Israel on their way to the Promised Land. When this strategy did not work, the women of Moab did a fine job of using their sensual wiles to distract and seduce the men of Israel. They literally led them into idol worship. Because of this, God declared Moabites to be enemies and they were not allowed to enter into the assembly of the Lord. The Israelites were not to even seek the peace and prosperity of the Moabites, and that was the end of that. Moabites were to be avoided at all cost. Moab was considered enemy territory. Nothing good could possibly come out of Moab.

Now there are a few things we need to consider here. The story goes that Elimelech and his family remained in Moab. I am sure after they got to Moab and considered the customs that were so foreign to their own, they had to question their choice. Did they really want their sons Mahlon (which means "sickly") and Chilion (which means "wasting away") to live in this society and assimilate to these people's habits that they knew were not pleasing to God? By their names we know that they were already susceptible to sickness and death. Their new environment could be detrimental, yet this couple's hunger told them they had no choice.

Man Fact:
Because men are fixers, under pressure they usually vote for the practical over the spiritual. It takes a woman to inspire them to seek God before listening to their own panic.

Many of us are this way. We know that we should not remain in the situation we are in, yet we stay in a dead-end relationship because something feels better than nothing. However, the price we pay is dear. Eventually the relationship comes to an end because God will not suffer it to continue. In the aftermath, we are assaulted by rejection and the realization of wasted time, emotions, and energy that we will never be able to retrieve. If we fell into sexual sin, a piece of our soul was left with that man, and we can never regain it. And the void he left behind will follow us into our next relationship. After too many of these repeat performances, we are simply an empty shell with nothing left to give should the right man come along.

It is important to your emotional well-being and health that you make an honest assessment of your situation. Is it conducive to you having the life and fulfillment you so deeply desire? Or are you merely slapping a Band-Aid over an untended wound, hoping you will feel better? We know if we do not deal with cuts properly, they can fester and infect our entire body. There is no bandage that can cover an empty or hurting heart. It must be brought to light, cleansed, and healed with time and the right attention. Loneliness must be put into perspective. You are greater than the feeling. Stop and take stock. It is a feeling that eventually passes. Though it may revisit you often, it does pass! Have a strategy for what you will do when loneliness visits. One strategy should be to not get involved in unfruitful relationships or those that bear the wrong kind of fruit. Do not compromise your morals and standards because a feeling urges you to do so.

Feed your hunger with things that build you up and make you a better you, from digging into the Word of God to various activities that stimulate, invigorate, and fulfill you. Focus on relationships and friendships that nurture you and build you up. Actually, this is a great time to assess what you want out of life and get busy making those things happen. I will share more on this later. The bottom line is we can waste away without realizing it when we stay in the wrong place, the wrong situation, the wrong relationship.

Personal Confession:

I will not allow myself to remain in situations that are not fruitful or contributing to my well-being physically, emotionally, or spiritually.

The Biological Clock Issue

Now, next on the list is a biggie. Let's deal with the biological clock issue. As women, most of us have pictured a child in our future. It is only natural to desire children. As the years go by, we begin to glance at the timer and decide our best childbearing years are running out. As our chance for having children narrows, we begin to take the matter out of God's hands and into our own. This is a time when many women become vulnerable in their panic and decide to just have a child and not wait for a husband. Not a good idea!

"Why not?" you ask. Because you are fooling yourself, that's why. When those pregnancy hormones kick in, a woman begins to nest. This means she longs not just for a child, but for a mate and a happy home. She is horrified and mortified, however, to find out that the "baby daddy" does not feel the same. That is when "mama drama" begins. Loading on the guilt that he should want to be with his child as a full-time father only deepens his resentment. Never mind that it took two to tango. You just ruined his life by introducing a major burden he did not plan for or want.

Enter the beautiful, bouncing baby and the reality of all that it takes to nurture a life. You realize you can forget about life ever being the same. Feelings of rejection are compounded with fear and being completely overwhelmed. Of course, this beautiful child brings you joy, but the sobering fact of worrying about provision and both of your futures can be frightening. Everyone knows someone in this situation. And what can you do except offer a helping hand?

Small wonder God's plan says to wait until marriage for sex. This can also apply to raising children when we will have the support system we need to maintain a thriving household. Children are work, and God never intended for a woman to have to go it alone. Though He promises to be a father to the fatherless and offers grace for our mistakes, the issues of single-parenting are still issues that do not go away. Children wrestle with their identity: *Why isn't their father there? Doesn't he love them? And if he doesn't, what does that mean?*

Even in our liberal society, nothing seems to have changed. A woman still wrestles with the stigma of being a single mother. Will another man be willing to marry her now that she has a child or children? Or worse yet, she has the trepidation about how the man she marries will deal with her child. The worst-case alternative is to marry a man just because she feels she needs a father for her children and subjects herself to a marriage that falls short of her dreams and desires.

Then there are the children. Sons grow up without seeing a living example of how men behave as a husband or the head of a household. They carry these issues into relationships with women and often fail miserably. Daughters grow up not knowing how to have healthy relationships with men and do all the wrong things to receive love from men. The wrong agenda always leads to less-than-desirable results. Questions, worries, and regrets abound. It is a heavy load for one person to bear. In the midst of the hunger for love, these things are not thought out and the heart justifies seeking after what it wants, ignoring the consequences.

Man Fact:
A man will take whatever you give him; therefore, consider the cost before giving.

This is not a slam against single mothers. God is not a God of condemnation. He stands with the fatherless and the husbandless and makes provision for them. I can personally attest to this. After my mother and father went their separate ways, my mother's family stepped up to the task of contributing to my upbringing. I was surrounded by love and never even knew anything was missing in my life. Several years later, my mother married Mr. McKinney, who became a wonderful father to me and treated me as his own. After rather miraculous events, my relationship with my natural father, Mr. Hammond, was restored and we remain close.

I ended up with two wonderful fathers in my life—a double blessing—who bore the responsibility of directing me and providing for me without any strife. This is not always the case. Sometimes there is no happy ending and the burden to be both mother and father, to be a child's everything, is left up to the mother. I tip my hat to those women who are able to master this challenge. I simply recommend that this should not be your conscious choice.

The questions you must ask yourself in these moments are, "Is my hunger for a child real or imagined?" "Do I want a child because it does something for *me?*" Or, "Do I want a child because I want to pour myself out for the sake of this precious life?" This is the spirit of a true mother. It is not about you; it is about the life of a child. If you can truly say that you want to give your life for another, then I highly recommend mentoring, fostering, or adopting. That is, if it is not about you. But even here, for the permanent situations, I recommend approaching them with much thought and prayer. Decide if you are doing this because you do not believe that God will *ever* bring you a mate, or because you feel very strongly in your spirit that it is the call of your life to nurture someone who would be lost without your love. Search your heart and be very honest. Remember, hunger passes.

The Self-made Life

But back to the main issue. Doing it yourself always results in the death of something: your dreams, the plans you had made for your life, joy, peace, fulfillment. Elimelech, the leader of the crew that went down to Moab, was the first to die. Could it be that he did not do well in Moab either? I doubt that was the problem. After all, Naomi, his wife, did not die or even get sick. Perhaps he was sick at heart and wasted away in his soul until his body followed suit. When we move out of place, out of time, out of God's perfect design, we lose pieces of ourselves that we can never get back. We spend the rest of our lives compensating for the losses incurred from bad choices.

Personal Confession:

I will consider my heart condition carefully and not be ruled by it. I will make sound judgments and choices not based on my cravings but on my gifts and my purpose so I may fulfill my destiny according to God's design.

What we must bear in mind is that other people besides ourselves are affected. Those around us are asked to pay a price as well. Naomi ended up a widow. Her sons were left without a father to be their leader and example. The patriarch, the head of the family, was gone and would not be replaced. God is the great Restorer, but why go through the unnecessary grief of experiencing losses if we do not have to?

Choose the journey you want to take and stick to the path ordained by God. The quick fix only brings about more problems in the long run. Decide to trust God to make provision for you when it comes to love, and you will never go wrong. The old folks used to say, "He may not come when you want Him, but He's right on time." That is the gospel truth.

Remember, there is a season for everything. There is a time for planting, so sow carefully. There is also a time to let what you have planted grow. During this time, it may seem as if nothing is happening, but deep beneath the surface, beyond what your eye can see, something is indeed going on! The roots of what you have planted are digging down deep. In due season, those seeds will sprout and bear marvelous fruit.

What would you like to harvest: joy, contentment, fulfillment? Then do not let your hunger manipulate the seed. You have been given the power of choice, a great gift from God. You can choose life or death, blessing or curses. Your decisions will dictate what you receive. If you are like Elimelech, confessing that God is your King, you will have to trust Him with timing as well as provision for your life.

Check your attitude toward God. Do you believe He loves you? Do you believe He wants the best for you? Do you believe He knows what is best for you? When you hire a painter, you do not help him paint the walls. No matter how long it takes him to finish his task, you leave him to do it because you believe he knows what he is doing. Sometimes waiting on God is like watching paint dry. It is hard to see progress on the surface because there is nothing visibly changing before you, and yet, the results are lasting once the paint has set. If you are struggling with the concept of God's goodness, this needs to be your first area of concentration. Settle in your heart that God is good all the time and wants you to experience lasting love and fulfillment even more than you do. This is crucial to your spiritual and emotional health. If you never get this settled between yourself and the Lover of your soul, then truly your faith will wither and you will die. And above all things, His desire for you is to live.

Ponder This

- What things do you do to compensate for the love hunger you feel?

- What healthier choices can you make for yourself that will lead to peace and joy?

- Are you driven by what you want to *receive* or what you want to *give*?

- What choices can you make to redirect your desires so that you will bless other people as well as yourself?

The thief comes only to steal and kill and destroy; I have come that they may have life, and have it to the full (John 10:10).

3

Love at Any Cost

And she [Naomi] was left, and her two sons. Now they took wives of the women of Moab: the name of the one was Orpah, and the name of the other Ruth....Then both Mahlon and Chilion [Naomi's sons] also died.

RUTH 1:3-5 NKJV

$\mathcal{W}$e are about to tackle what we should settle for when we have limited our options by our own design. If Moab was the environment Naomi's sons were in, what other choice could they make regarding wives? Mahlon and Chilion ended up marrying women from Moab: Orpah (meaning "neck") and Ruth (meaning "friendship"). "Sickly" marries "friendship" (that which should have been able to nurture), and "wasting away" marries "neck" (that which should have been able to be a support) but marriage is not enough to nurture these two men to health. Eventually they die.

It becomes clear that marriage is not the answer in and of itself. Marriage is never the solution to our problems. As a matter of fact, it could make matters worse if our issues are not dealt with first. If we are sickly in our attitude toward life and love, and wasting away because we believe we are incomplete without a man, nothing will change after the words "I do" are uttered. It is hard to imagine this, but an even greater loneliness awaits you after securing a mate and discovering he cannot help you feel any better about yourself. Many women shrivel up and die daily within the confines of what they just knew would be the safe haven of marriage.

These two men married women that the law told them they should not even *consider*. They were supposed to marry women from among their own people, women who had the same culture, background, and belief system. The struggle for two people to become one is usually less severe if they agree on most things starting out. Mahlon and Chilion's hunger led them to compromise their standards, believing they would find life. Instead, they died slow, painful deaths, which is what happens to most relationships of this nature.

For believers in Christ, the issue of being "unequally yoked" is not about race, but about spiritual culture and experiences. Both of you can be Christians and still be unequally yoked. Are you both on the same path, walking toward the light, choosing to obey God because you are committed to living according to His Word? That is the big question. Two cannot walk together unless they have agreed to do so (Amos 3:3). The bottom line is this: If you are not walking in the same direction in life, you will end up going separate ways. Whether you are a Christian or not, aligning yourself in a committed relationship with a man who does not agree with your values and basic belief systems will be problematic throughout the life of your marriage. It will never be harmonious. Neither of you will be equipped to continue in a home where you disagree more than you agree.

Many women who have married men who did not hold their same spiritual passion spend the rest of their marriages going to church alone and asking other people to pray that their husband will come to a place of embracing a relationship with God. They are lonely and unfulfilled because they feel a gaping chasm between themselves and their husbands on the grounds of what they do not share. What seemed worthy of the risk before the wedding day gives them room to pause afterward. And let's not even speak about what happens after children enter the picture and become affected by their father's lack of interest in spiritual things.

For single Christian women, a great and real concern is there are not enough men in the church. What are their options? Let me tell you what is *not* an option: missionary dating. That would be what we are doing when we decide to recruit and save an unbelieving man. Most of us have had a missionary dating experience, or maybe even many.

Man Fact:
A man will never feel the need to change if you accept him and commit to him with the full knowledge that he does not embrace your values.

Even I have to lift a guilty finger on this one and confess that I, too, had to learn the hard way. Why are we instructed to avoid being unequally yoked? Because God knew the nature of the beasts that were harnessed together.

Though we convince ourselves that we can influence the man to come to Christ, the sad truth is, in most cases, this is not what occurs. Lack of success is usually due to the inability of the woman to maintain her standards and not compromise her ethics or position. This is what happens when you yoke a weak ox to a strong one. The strong one is not able to pull the weaker ox to match his pace. The strong ox then compensates for the weakness of the other ox by stepping back and slowing its pace. After a while, its muscles that are no longer being used begin to grow weak, and he ends up in the same shape as the ox he was joined to.

The Valley of Compromise

It is just as easy to fall in love with a nonbeliever as it is to fall in love with a believer. The nonbeliever might score extra points in some areas if we are really being truthful here. Let's be honest on how the relationship plays out with a woman who is smitten with a man who does not have her same spiritual commitment. She has a tendency to compromise, not sexually at first, but conversationally. She decides that she is not going to push her beliefs on him, so she remains quiet. She does not speak up when the conversation travels down a path it should not. She does not say things she should and says things she should not. She almost ends up apologizing at times for what she believes so he will not be "uncomfortable." It is interesting that she will sacrifice her own comfort level for someone who has no respect for what she believes.

After the conversation gets watered down, her habits begin to decline. In an effort to prove she is flexible, she misses church or Bible class. She stops being transparent with her friends because she does not want to be held accountable. Once she becomes disconnected, it is easy to take the next step: physically relaxing. Entering into a sexual relationship before marriage brings condemnation. Once she has compromised enough, her conscience becomes seared to the point where she begins to justify her actions.

Meanwhile, she fails to realize she has lost this man's respect. Even the world is impressed when a woman can stand up for what she believes without cracking. In this example, the man does not find the woman at all impressive. She talked a good game in the beginning, but in the end he wore her down. Oh well, the challenge is now over...next! It's simply a matter of time.

The Bible clearly shows that whenever people compromised with those who did not share their knowledge and their love for

God, the relationship ended in death. This could be death of joy, peace, and fulfillment, or perhaps even a physical sacrifice was made. The best example of this is Samson. When Samson married a Philistine woman, the affair ended in betrayal and a revengeful bloodbath. Later, when he got involved with a Philistine prostitute, he almost got caught in a death trap. People were lying in wait to kill him after he emerged from the prostitute's home. Even after that, he still had not learned his lesson. He ended up living with the infamous Delilah, another Philistine woman. This relationship not only led to his being blinded, but also to bondage and eventually death! Though God lovingly redeemed him before he died, perhaps he would have been around a little longer had he not made the fatal choices that he did. He just *lo-o-oved* those foreign women! Sadly, more than he loved God. In the end, what he loved most did not love him back.

How many times are we blinded by the emotions that flood us when we are with someone who makes us feel good, no matter how bad the situation may be for us? We are not foolish for making a mistake—only for refusing to learn from it. How often will we deliberately walk into relationships we know can go nowhere to assuage our hunger? Some women have conditioned themselves to think, "Well, this is just something to do for now," while inwardly knowing they want so much more. Self-deception quickly gives way to unnecessary pain when the relationship ends and we are faced with the overwhelming truth that our words and emotions did not really match. It is time to take control of our lives, ladies, and guard our hearts so we do not grow sickly and waste away after enduring disappointment after disappointment. Stop settling for less than the best for yourself. Stop nibbling at appetizers you do not even like because you do not know when the main course is coming. Safeguard your emotions and save room in your heart for the real thing.

Despite what your eyes see, God is not limited in His reserve of men whom He has set aside for uncompromising women. Perhaps there is a test that must be passed first. How do you deal with your love hunger? Are you willing to become a disciplined eater? With whom are you hanging out? Where are you going? All these factors could be limiting your options. I am not saying that you should not have any friends who do not agree with your beliefs or lifestyle. After all, Jesus made dangerous friends that the Pharisees, the religious watchdogs of the day, disapproved of. Yet He did not make these dangerous friends His close disciples. His inner circle was reserved for those who were looking for the truth and shared his passion for the things of God. He talked with those of the secular world, ate with them, and nurtured relationships with them for the sole purpose of turning their hearts to God. If your goal in your relationship with a man who does not embrace what you believe is to draw his heart toward *you* and not toward *God*, you will lose on both counts.

Personal Confession:

I will not compromise my standards and settle for someone who does not walk in agreement with my values just to have a man in my life. I will hold out for the one who is right for me.

The Value of Love

Perhaps part of the problem is not knowing who you are or recognizing your value. This, coupled with a healthy dose of not trusting God to give you your heart's desire, is enough to make you settle for anything! As I have often taught, God makes many references comparing us to precious jewels—rare rubies whose price exceeded all other gems at the time. If you consider your worth to be that of a priceless diamond, whose flaws can only be seen by a master craftsman through a high-powered magnifying lens, then you can rest assured that is exactly how God values you. These types of diamonds are not left out in the open for the general public to see. They are kept in the owner's safe. Only people who know specifically what they are looking for are exposed to these incredible stones. They are not in a setting yet because each stone is designed individually according to its worth and weight. The greater the weight, the stronger the setting must be to hold it.

For larger stones, the recommendation is usually made for them to be set in platinum—the hardest metal in which a stone can be set. It is a rarer metal and used in 90 percent of its pure form. Only ten percent of other metals are added to it in order to make the setting hold. Gold is a softer metal. This means up to 40 percent of other metals are added to make it hard enough to hold a stone; therefore, it is not pure gold. The gold can soften from the heat of our hands and bend. Sometimes the prongs will loosen and the stone will be lost or have to be reset. What we as women want is a setting that is pure and strong enough to hold our hearts securely.

In essence, the setting (that would be the man), is just as important as the stone (that would be you). If the setting is not up to supporting and protecting the stone, your union could be short-lived! A true jeweler knows the worth of his stones and will not discount them. If you knew the true worth of your heart, your love, and your life, you would be just as uncompromising about casting your pearls before those who do not recognize your worth. You cannot get angry when swine trample over valuable fare because they are used to slop and leftovers. Whatever makes its way into their pen is treated the same. I have had to backtrack and release some men I held in unforgiveness for a long time and take the blame for the outcome of the relationship upon myself. In retrospect, I ignored God's advice and the nudging of the Holy Spirit that this man was not right for me and proceeded to try to make him right. It never works. If he does not fit from the beginning, he never will. It is like buying a dress that is too small in hopes of losing weight. That dress usually remains in the closet with the tag still on it.

The same could be said for designer clothing. At its source, it never goes on sale, especially if it is a couture garment (something that has been exactly fitted to the wearer). No one else will be able to wear that piece except the person for whom it was made. We were designed by God to fit one man, to fill the gap in his rib. Of course, we could fit with many men, but one will fit better than most. If we want the best mate for our lives, we must be willing to understand our own uniqueness and wait for the right fit.

Now there is no perfect man, but there is one who will be better suited for loving you and dealing with all the delicate areas of your heart and spirit. He will be handcrafted by God from the day of his birth to embrace you and fit just right. The imperfections that remain will be deliberately left by God. Why? Because it is the rough edges of two people that sharpen one another like nothing else can (Proverbs 27:17). If we allow ourselves to be used to temper the uncultivated parts of

Man Fact:
A man will only feel he has gotten a prize if he has to pay a price for it.

each other's spirit, we both emerge as better people with a greater capacity for love and victorious living.

How do we find out what our value is? By looking into the Word of God and seeing what He thinks of us. If the King of kings says we have value, we better believe it! He says that we are fearfully and wonderfully made. What does that mean exactly? It means He had tremendous respect for His own creation, that even He had a sense of awe as He oversaw us being formed in our mother's womb. An even greater fact is the sacrifice He made to rescue us from our own sinful nature, literally from ourselves. The price He paid to ransom us from the grip of the enemy of our souls is inconceivable: the life of His own Son, Jesus. How many of us would be willing to allow our child to be killed to save someone else?

With so great a price tag on our lives, how can we allow those who do not realize or acknowledge our worth to claim our hearts, to abuse and use us in a manner that causes us to question our value? Ask yourself, *Would God treat me the way this man is treating me?* If the answer is no, cut him off at the pass! Women, it is time for us to acknowledge our worth and not waste our time with those who simply "don't get it." Are your standards too high? Indeed not! God designs big plans for us in every area of our life. Most of the time we think too small.

Do not ever apologize for keeping a standard; instead, let it be your guidepost. Quietly lift and separate your options and decide if the man standing before you is conducive to how you see your life moving forward. If he is more of a distraction than an asset and is causing you to stray from your course, release him and move on. Just because he is not the one for you does not mean he will not be perfect for someone else. Be a sister who speaks the truth in love to him. Do this in a way so he will be a better man for the next woman he meets.

I know I have groomed several men to be great mates for other women, even though they were not a good fit for me. Sometimes they *were* wonderful for me, but I was not good for them. Be honest with yourself and decide if you can be the complement he needs. Do not be selfish and keep someone hanging on because all of your needs are being met. Love must be a two-way offering. Both people should be blessed in the giving.

The young men I mentioned earlier in this chapter, Mahlon and Chilion, died in a place where they did not belong, caught up in relationships they should not have had. Though God is able to redeem anything, more often than not when two people are involved with conflicting wills, death is the outcome of the ill-fitted relationship. Something is not necessarily better than nothing if that something will eventually kill you or the things you hold dear. Take the time to list what you truly want from life and stick to your list. Do not allow love hunger to talk you into taking an appetizer that leaves no room for the real meal God wants to serve you. Remember, God's design for love is to fill you with life-giving fruit that in turn gives life to others.

Ponder This

- How do you find yourself compromising when your faith for a mate runs low?

- What steps can you take to rebuild your faith and fortify yourself to wait for the one who is worthy of you?

- What self-worth issues do you have? How do they cause you to compromise your standards?

He who is full loathes honey, but to the hungry even what is bitter tastes sweet (Proverbs 27:7).

4
The Winds of Change

*When she heard in Moab that the LORD had come to the
aid of his people by providing food for them, Naomi and
her daughters-in-law prepared to return home from there.
With her two daughters-in-law she left the place where she
had been living and set out on the road that would take
them back to the land of Judah.*

RUTH 1:6-7

Rumor has it that patience wins the game of life. Naomi gets
wind of the fact that the people she left behind in pursuit of a
full tummy are still alive, eating, and none the worse for wear in
spite of staying put. She, on the other hand, had suffered great
losses in the land of her own undoing. The journeys we choose
for ourselves, when we think life is not going as it should, often
lead us down a detour even further away from our desires. Those
who stay on course, no matter how much their longings cause
their spiritual stomachs to growl, are able to smile at the
journey's end, minus the scars we bear.

Oh, how I can relate! I recall an incident that was a marker
for me in my own single life. After establishing a relationship
with Christ and making the commitment to be obedient to His
Word, the initial zeal of my newfound faith wore off and I found

myself challenged in my personal life. Before I came to the Lord, I had always had a man in my life. As a matter of fact, I was living with someone before I became a Christian. His death was what propelled me into the arms of Christ. My new lifestyle definitely affected my dating habits. None of the men I went out with could wrap his head around the concept of celibacy. Small wonder because none of them was claiming to be a Christian! Needless to say, after a while my phone did not ring as often. No longer hanging out, dancing the night away, and meeting fun guys who never meant to be serious was not something I missed. However, I did miss having someone in my life to share my heart with (as much as I knew how at the time, that is). So I made a bargain with God. I told Him I could live a celibate life for exactly one year, and after that I would not be responsible for my actions! I am sure He got a big laugh out of my directive. I had some nerve back then. I am sure He celebrated my commitment to even that, which was a far leap from skipping over any page in my Bible that I thought was going to tell me that sex before marriage was a no-no. For some strange reason, I thought if I did not read about this, I would not have to be obedient to it. Fortunately, I could not get away from my own spirit where the law of God was already written on my heart, giving me an instinctual knowledge of right and wrong according to the One who had created me in the first place.

After making this proclamation, I made my second deal with my omniscient Father. He should save a famous musician that I had dated and give him to me as a husband. I would be willing to wait for him and consider no other man as long as God would hurry up. Well, He did not pay attention to any of my plea bargaining, and my misplaced expectations made the next several years bitterly painful ones. I was determined to stick it out with God, but I cannot say I did so joyfully. Actually, I became the worst religious nightmare. I loudly judged people who compromised their lives and "lived in sin," not because I truly wanted them to walk in victory with God, but because I was jealous! Yes, in hindsight I felt they were allowed to enjoy themselves and get away with it while I could not. I lived in fear of God's wrath and the consequences of my sin, even though I was not sure what they would be. You see, in the back of my heart I harbored the hope that if I was a good little Christian "do-bee," God would give me exactly what I wanted. I would score major brownie points with Him, and He would be so impressed by my goodness that He would have to cooperate with my agenda. But if I was "bad," I could kiss my dreams good-bye.

But alas, I had a hard lesson to learn. God did not owe me anything for my obedience. He does not bless us because of outward actions. He blesses as He is moved by our inner attitudes and His own determinations of what is good for us. He had already given the greatest blessing of all, the sacrifice of His Son, Jesus, for my silly sake. How dare I think He owed me anything else! The reality was *I* owed *Him* my obedience. That was the *least* I could do. Never did I stop to consider that He had promised to give me only good and perfect gifts. Believe me, though that musician was nice, he was not a good and perfect gift for me. I gave it a valiant effort anyway. I waited and waited, choosing to believe God would see things my way eventually. No one could convince me to release this self-deception.

Personal Confession:

I will not try to force other people to walk in my light, but will apply myself to being joyfully obedient to the path upon which I have been called to walk.

Meanwhile, one of my closest friends, the lady who taught me all the spiritual ropes when I was new in the faith, was engaged to be married. I recall saying to her, "Wow, I can't believe you remained celibate for seven years!" My little mind could not conceive of denying my flesh that long! She sweetly answered, "Well, you never know. The Lord might make you wait that long." To which I quickly replied without a thought, "Oh no, He won't, because I would backslide!" Those words would haunt me seven years later when I finally decided that God was never going to give me a husband. My self-fulfilling prophecy caused me to plummet to the depths of rebellion. I decided it was time to take things into my own hands and fulfill my own longings. I was not going to let the next potential candidate for love get away. I had done it God's way, and He had failed me. It was time to take my body, as well as my desires, back into my own hands. I turned back on my commitment to celibacy and, to my dismay, found myself more miserable than ever—on several levels.

First, my religious face was broken. I did not realize how much I had become wrapped up in pride about being celibate for so long. I am sure that was apparent to everyone else around me! Like an athlete who fails to keep his record due to one wrong move, I was disappointed by my failure. I could no longer preach to other people and berate those who had failed because I was in the same boat. It was devastating to finally understand, "There, but for the grace of God, go I."

Secondly, after obsessing over this area of my life for so long, the experience was not as fulfilling as I had imagined. I could not enjoy myself because all I kept thinking of was how God felt. Was He disappointed in me? What had I done to our relationship? I truly loved God. He had been faithful to me, supplying my needs through thick and thin. As a matter of fact, I could honestly say He had answered all of my prayers except this one for a mate. Bowed over by guilt and condemnation, the little bit of joy I had quickly ran down the drain. Meanwhile, all of my friends who had been toeing the line and being obedient had much more peace than I did, even though they had their moments of loneliness. I hid from them, too ashamed to reach out for counsel and help. I was now lonelier than ever.

It seemed the grace that had covered me and given me the power to keep myself from the grip of sexual temptation had evaporated, and now it was a struggle for me to stay pure. How would I ever find my way back to the safe place I had in the center of God's will?

In the midst of my shame, a realization dawned. Pride in my own works had blinded me to the fact that the only reason I had been able to say no to temptation was because of God, not myself. The moment I decided I was angry at Him and decided to take my life back into my own hands, He lifted His protective covering just long enough for me to see what I was really made of. It was not a pretty picture. After many tears and a deep, heartfelt repentance, I struggled to receive the forgiveness that God gave. And that was the easy part. For far longer than I care to admit, I held myself hostage in the prison of my own unforgiveness. The way back to peace and fulfillment seemed farther away than ever.

Starting from Scratch

How do we get back on track when we have taken an unhealthy detour? Well, the first thing we need to do is own up to our actions and be strong enough to say we had a hand in creating our drama. If we are truly honest, all the red flags were waving. We simply refused to acknowledge them and hoped things would work out to our liking if we continued to pursue what or whom we wanted. Our Bible heroine Naomi did not claim ownership very well in the story I have been sharing. Even though she had the good sense to go back home, on two occasions along the way she blamed her lot in life on the Lord, without ever owning up to the fact that she was the one who had moved, not God. She was the one who had broken His rules and was now in a state of dismay and bitterness.

Personal Confession:

I will not cast blame, but will take responsibility for my decisions and mistakes, being honest with God and myself.

In my situation, I had to face the fact that I was wrong, a victim of my own poor decisions. Therefore, I was responsible for change taking place in my life. I had to collect myself and make some resolution. Was I going to remain paralyzed in my situation, or was I going to move forward? I decided to pull myself together and make the journey back to where I had come from with a new attitude, no matter how difficult the path. Perhaps your journey into the depths of compromise is not as deep as mine was, but you have strayed off the path of kingdom living in your heart. Sometimes our bodies are in the kingdom, but our minds are on the other side of the world. We go through the motions of holiness without emotion or passion, no longer motivated by our love for God. Out of duty, we toe the line, devoid of a grateful heart or a worshipful attitude. Not being a cheerful giver of yourself is just as bad as outwardly acting out what you are really feeling inside. After all, God knows your heart.

On the other hand, perhaps you have never made the commitment to love God or be obedient to His Word. But you are sick and tired of being sick and tired of experiencing countless unfulfilling relationships. You are left feeling empty and used, wondering if you will ever find true love. In or out of the kingdom of God, the answer is the same. Want different results? Do something different. Naomi made the crucial decision to leave the place where she had been. This is the first step to getting a new life and changing your circumstances.

A Turn for the Better

I decided to get out of my situation. I told Mr. Man I could no longer live a compromised life and I was ending the relationship. I am not saying it did not hurt. What I *am* saying is that there were things more important to me: my relationship with God, my peace of mind, my spiritual and emotional state. I chose to do what I had to do to get back to what I knew I could not live without. The first thing I did was face my weaknesses and set boundaries to help myself stay on track. I knew that if I left sweets lying around, I would have to take a nibble; therefore, I had to clean out the cupboard. I made the decision that, though I may have friends or associates who did not believe what I believed or hold the same standards for their life, I would no longer date men who did not.

Man Fact:
"Worldly" men have no problem dating church girls—they find them a delightful challenge. Just remember: Their intentions do not match yours.

Examine your relationships. Do your friends and associates hold the same standard for living that you do? If not, rethink how much time you should spend with them. Though Jesus made quite a few unorthodox friends, they were not in His inner circle. The only ones in His inner circle were those who were seeking to walk in the same direction He was headed. If you are trying to live one way, and your closest friends or the man in your life live another, you will always struggle with discontent. Your resolve will be weakened, and you will find yourself trying without success to navigate down a slippery path. No woman can serve two masters—she will love one and hate the other (Matthew 6:24). The Spirit of God and the flesh will never be friends or abide peacefully together in the same house. One of them is going to have to go.

I forced myself to make no provision for my flesh to rule over me, and instead chose to be accountable to a few spiritually mature friends who could speak the truth in love to me without being judgmental. And I stopped being judgmental of other people. I was now armed with a greater understanding for how someone could easily fall if not watching her p's and q's, or not sticking close to the One who could give her overcoming strength.

I then focused my attention on rebuilding my faith in God by studying specific areas of Scripture that helped me to know how much He loved me, the plans He had for my life, and how He only wanted what was best for me. If these things were really true, then I would have to trust Him in the mate department. If He knew how to give good gifts in every other area of my life, why could I not trust Him with this one thing?

Was it because I harbored some deep fear that He would force me to accept someone who was ugly, boring, or just not my "type"? Why did I think God had bad taste? All of these were questions I had to settle within myself. To rebuild my faith, I turned not only to the Word of God, but also to living examples in my life. I looked at the happy married couples I knew. All the men were wonderful men that I admired. Obviously, none of my girlfriends had been the unwilling recipient of a man from God she could not stand!

Next, I began to nurture a grateful heart by being thankful for what I already had in my life: rich friendships, a supportive family, and a wonderful network of people who believed as I believed, and who found all kinds of interesting activities in which to be involved. I devoted myself to nurturing those relationships and living in the moment. I focused on living in the present, instead of

Personal Confession:

I will choose to be grateful for the blessings and good things I have at hand right now and not allow my desire for a different future to rob me of living in the present to the fullest.

always worrying about what the future would hold and how much longer I must go it alone.

I believe that Ruth threw her future into the arms of God and decided to take the sure path by going with Naomi. Naomi was someone Ruth knew and loved, someone she could care for in the present. She also chose to embrace Naomi's customs, her people, and her God. Ruth was taking a risk, and she knew it. What if the people in Judah did not accept her? She could not dwell on that. She just knew hanging out in Moab hoping she would get another husband was not the way to go. There had to be more to life than putting all of her hopes on finding a man.

Obviously, her sister-in-law Orpah did not feel the same way. When Naomi told them they might fare better returning to their mothers' homes in Moab than going with her because she could not guarantee them husbands in Judah, Orpah promptly made her decision to stay where she was. We never hear anything else about Orpah. I wonder if she ever got another husband, or if she eked out the rest of her days in her mother's house regretting her decision?

Those who live a life dedicated solely to finding a husband usually fade into oblivion. Because this is their only focus, nothing else in life becomes significant enough to note. These people do not usually invest their energies into nurturing their gifts or become involved in activities that could take them away from the goal of finding a man. Should they actually get a man, their entire identity becomes wrapped up in the relationship. They drop the friends who patiently listened to their single woes, and nothing much is heard from them again unless something goes wrong in the relationship. The percentage of those who remain happy in this type of arrangement is very low. They usually find their expectations of what a man would add to their world to be misplaced at best, leaving them more unhappy in a relationship than they were when they did not have one. They might even decide they just got the wrong man and go in pursuit of another...and another...with each relationship having the same outcome.

Those who never stop to take a look at themselves as a part of the problem will allow disillusionment to paralyze them from pursuing purposeful living. The reality of the situation is this: Putting life on hold until you have a man is a bad idea. It is time to get a life. You can move now or move later, but move you must. Nothing will happen until you get over yourself and make a move to get past your present mental attitude and on to what will truly bring you happiness and fulfillment.

Deciding to leave where you are is one thing, but getting back on the right path toward the heart of God and healthy living is another. It will take willpower to stick to your plan when you do not see an immediate change in your circumstances or your joy level. You must determine to stay on the path daily, keeping the bigger picture in mind: peace, joy, and fulfillment that cannot be taken away by anything or anybody. Leaving behind unhealthy habits, relationships that are not going any-where, unvictorious mind-sets, and even friends who feed you the wrong advice is a must to get on the path that will lead you to where you want to be in life.

One last thing: Do not romanticize the past. When Naomi returned to her hometown and her friends called her by name, she told them to call her Mara (meaning "bitter") instead, because the Lord had made life very bitter for her. She said she had left Bethlehem full but was returning home empty. But I thought they left because of a famine! How could they be hungry and full at the same time? Perhaps after she left and lived under worse circumstances, she came to realize that life had been better before. Although they did not have everything they wanted, she had her health and her family intact, which was indeed a full life. Now she was empty. Many times after the fact, we look back on a bad relationship when we are alone and cling to the one good moment we had, forgetting all the negative things that were not conducive to our long-term happiness. We are tempted to return to a bad situation rather than wait for a better one. Do not go there. Stay on track!

Leave the idols behind—the things you have clung to with a fervor, insisting that you will not be happy until you have what you want. Discarding these will free you to see where true hap-piness lies and, more often than not, it will not be where you expected. That, my sister, is the beauty of life's surprises once we surrender to being open to them.

Ponder This

- At present, where are you living emotionally?

- What false impressions or hopes are you clinging to that rob you of your peace?

- Are you willing to risk stepping out of your comfort zone to find the life you want?

- What is your main focus? If you knew you were never going to be married, what would you do differently with your life?

For whoever wishes to save his life will lose it; but whoever loses his life for My sake will find it (Matthew 16:25 NASB).

5
Knowing Your Season

So Naomi returned from Moab, accompanied by her
daughter-in-law Ruth, the young Moabite woman.
They arrived in Bethlehem at the beginning
of the barley harvest.

RUTH 1:22 NLT

If you stay on track, you will get to a place of new beginnings, hope, and fulfillment. But you have to walk it out. Do not try to go it alone; it is too difficult. Covenant to walk with someone who has the ability to encourage you when you are down and vice versa. Most importantly, stop and take stock of your life, and recognize the season you are in.

Discontentment usually comes from not understanding the purpose or the season of our lives. I have found that my reading audience spends more time worrying about why I am not married than I do. Marriage is not uppermost on my mind because I understand the season I am in. Right now, I am sowing seeds. My heartbeat, my greatest passion is to see women living and loving victoriously. Why is it such a passion for me? Because I was so miserable for so long that when I discovered the secrets to loving the life I was living, I just had to share them with other people. I never anticipated how my commitment to sharing this news would revolutionize my life or rearrange my priorities.

When the questions began about my marital status, some out of cattiness, some out of genuine concern, I had to stop for a moment to ponder why, because I had not really given it much thought. A husband is not and was not something I actively prayed for. I had, from time to time, actually met someone who was interesting and attempted to have a relationship. But when faced with the choice of finishing a chapter on a new book or going out to dinner, I chose to date my computer instead. I was frustrated when I had to divide my attention between a project and this man. Cute as he was, I just was not present. He felt it and I knew it. I realized it was not fair to see someone only when it was convenient for me. I would certainly be going against what I preached. As I consulted with God as to why I was at such odds, being ambivalent about having someone in my life, I was relieved to understand that I was in a different season of my life. For now, the call on my life was my first love. This season might change in the future, and I actually anticipate it will, but that is not where I am right now.

But enough about me. What about you? Think about where you are right now…in all honesty. Take a good, hard look at yourself—consider your life and where it seems to be taking you. What seeds are you planting in order to get the life and the love you want? Perhaps this is your season for self-development. What dreams have you put on reserve, hoping a relationship would save you from yourself? Are you waiting to be rescued, carried off to an exciting life? Perhaps the man who would be exciting to you would not be excited by you because you are not doing anything yourself. The key to attracting what you want is *being* what you want to attract. Remember, a man wants to be your hero, but he certainly does not want to be your oxygen.

That means you have to get busy! You have to have fulfilling activities already going on in your life.

Now is the time to cultivate your interests and gifts. Take full advantage of your freedom. You will never have more financial freedom or more time than right now. Spend it wisely, cultivating a well-rounded and fascinating life. Do not pursue different activities based on if there will be men you can meet. Select what truly intrigues you. It is the best way to meet people who have similar interests.

Personal Confession:

I will not rush through the seasons of my life, but will give my full attention to the tasks and opportunities at hand.

If you are a single parent, perhaps this is the season for raising your children and giving them your undivided attention. I know some of you did not want to hear that! After observing women who have chosen to focus on raising their children first, it seems the moment the children are gone or off to college, God sends a partner. Hmm, it is enough to make you wonder.

The issues that face us in today's world caution us to be extremely careful to whom we expose our children. It is also hard on their hearts when they are carried through a promising relationship that does not work out in the end. More than one heart can be broken in a home. I believe God honors women who take the time to understand the season they are in and apply themselves to it, knowing that it will soon pass. Children grow so quickly and are gone sooner than we are ready for them to be. After they leave the nest is the time to be free to rediscover love. Then it will be without the angst of involving your children until you are truly ready to be committed to one another.

In those cases where God knows a woman needs help, I believe He will send it. Help will be either in the form of her family and friends, or in a mate who will be committed to her children and treat them as his own. I have to say that my mother, after being separated from my father, Mr. Hammond, did consciously look for a man who would be a suitable father for me. She was blessed to meet Mr. McKinney, who adopted me and has always treated me as if I was his very own daughter. I also must interject that up to that time, I was not aware anything was missing in my life because I was surrounded by the love of my mother's extended family. Aunts, uncles, and grandparents took me in and raised me until my mother was in the position to take me back into her own home. When Mr. McKinney arrived, he came with a heart big enough to accommodate me, as well as the other children they had together.

However, not every woman experiences so happy an ending; therefore, walk softly and allow God to do the mate selection, especially when children are involved. Ask Him to send the support system and help you need in the meantime. And please, don't be afraid to ask for help, especially if you are the mother of a son. God will be a father to the fatherless, but no mother should try to be all things to her children. She was not created male; she was created female. Ask the Lord to put a solid male figure in your life who can be a godly role model to your children.

Single Focus

If you are not a single parent, keep in mind you are still in a season. While pondering what it is going to take for you to get what you want from God, consider the fact that God may want something from you! Perhaps He wants you to get into the flow of your destiny and fulfill your purpose before you meet your mate. If you do not, you might end up with the wrong partner.

A man once told me that men like to know what they are getting in a wife, and they do not like surprises. Though we all grow as we mature, we should be on the path toward our goals and dreams, having a clear vision of our

Man Fact:
Men do not like surprises! They like to know what they are getting into and make their choices accordingly; therefore, have all your cards out up front.

passions and the things we want to accomplish in life.

Now is the time to become single-focused. Decide what you want your life to look like and prepare your dreams. This is the time to be planting seeds for your future, knowing that life will change drastically at harvesttime. Willingness to allow you to live life to the fullest will be the ultimate test that a man must pass in your life and vice versa. He should be able to consider you in all your ways. I doubt very seriously if I had gotten married before I began my career as an author and speaker in full-time ministry, if the man I married would have been able to transition well. I still struggle with how much my life has changed. Gone are the long periods of languishing at home, entertaining friends, and spontaneously taking vacations. Instead, my life has evolved into a grueling schedule that even the hardy shudder to think of. It will indeed take a special man to deal with my life as it is, though I understand some adjustments will have to be made on my part in order to accommodate a meaningful relationship.

Marriage is so much more than an emotional bond. It becomes a business arrangement of sorts. Two people are called to be more than lovers, they must be partners as well. They must be able to support one another's vision and the call that is on their lives. Though every man and woman is not in full-time ministry, whatever their passion or vocation, they must be able to stand behind one another and champion one another's cause. It would help if you shared similar passions so you could be an active cheerleader, if not a willing assist. The only way you will know if this is true in your relationship is if both of you are actively living out the purpose for which you were created.

I still chuckle at the fact that the area of my life that was the greatest cause of pain has become the most powerful part of my ministry. Truly, if we release our desires and become focused on making the most of the season we are in, God can transform our distress and disappointment into present joy that will remain undisturbed, no matter how long it takes for the fruit we want to come into full bloom.

Now is the time to shout, "Carpe diem!" ("Seize the day!") Work on yourself while the only person you really have to worry about is you. Do you like your body? If not, now is the time to change eating habits, get into an exercise routine, or whatever it takes to become the you you want to be. Remember, when you feel good about yourself, other people will, too. What about your finances? Are you in debt? Now is the time to get out of debt while there is just one of you. Take the time to clear your decks and save money so you are ready for a new life with new responsibilities and expenses.

Are you waiting for a man to purchase a house for you? What if he never comes? Speak to a financial counselor and get your affairs in order. Purchase something to rent out or to live in if you can, and begin to build a future for yourself. A man will be happier about embracing a woman who has her financial act together than one who looks like she might be a drain on what he possesses.

Is there something you have always wanted to try? Now is the time when you are not bound by sharing finances or time. Go for it. Experiment with life now while you have no one else to subject to your exper-imentations. If you have ever considered living in another city, you are free to go. Now is the time to be daring, to go where you have never gone, and do what you have never done. Open yourself to a world of possibilities and have the time of your life.

Man Fact: A man is attracted to a woman who is not only interested, but interesting. He wants to know he will be inspired and stimulated to higher levels by your presence in his life.

You can be the one to mobilize all of your single friends. Start a travel club. Do a club savings program and pick a destination. Experience life to the fullest. This time of freedom will last only for a while. Having a partner might change some things so that it will not be possible to be so footloose and fancy-free. Why not take stock of what you could have and make the most of this season?

The funny thing about seasons is that they may feel as if they will go on forever, especially if the one you are in is not your favorite season. But it is inevitable: This, too, shall pass. If you are faithful to embrace your season and plant the right seed, your moment of harvest is sure to come. When it does, it will yield your heart's desire.

Ponder This

- What things are you waiting to do until you get your mate? If these are things that you can do alone, what is stopping you?

- Make a list of things you would like to try and places you would like to go. Map out a game plan for how you will accomplish these things.

- What season are you in? What purpose do you think God is trying to guide you into before marriage?

There is a time for everything, and a season for every activity under heaven (Ecclesiastes 3:1).

6
Making Life Work

Then she [Ruth] left, and went and gleaned in the field after the
reapers. And she happened to come to the part of the field
belonging to Boaz, who was of the family of Elimelech.

RUTH 2:3 NKJV

The plot thickens! While Ruth was not exactly looking where
she was going, she definitely landed in the right place. In a field
at harvesttime, her needs were about to be met in ways she had
not imagined. What was on Ruth's mind when she headed for
that field? Survival. Eating. That's all. She did not go looking for
a husband. She did not even expect to find one. Sometimes
when we cast our expectations to the wind without bitterness
and discontent, I believe God is even more motivated to deliver
the secret desires of our heart.

Ruth went to pick up the leftover grain being dropped by
reapers in the fields. In other words, she was willing to work with
what was available to her. We can either pin our hopes on the
way we would like things to be, or we can work with what is in
front of us. God has promised that if we are faithful with little,
He will make us ruler over much (Luke 19:17).

How do we make our lives purposeful while we are alone? By
applying ourselves to all we can do as singles. It is time to break

the mold and cast down the misconceptions people have of singles. One popular assessment is that singles spend all of their time bemoaning the fact they are single and fail to be productive. I do not want to wear that mantle, do you? On and on it goes: Singles are engrossed with themselves…they do not take advantage of all their freedom affords…they are fiscally irresponsible, major consumers of anything that amuses from toys to clothing in order to appease their loneliness. Is this really true? If so, it is never too late to change.

Sometimes what we have to work with in our lives does not look like much; however, it is a place to start. The Bible story says that Ruth decided to go gleaning and *happened* upon the field of Boaz. She did not even know she had selected a prime location. She not only found the field of Boaz, she also found favor in his sight.

I have to stop here. Many women have the order backwards: finding a man first, making a life second. The ironic thing is that it is in the making of life that the man is found. A friend of mine comes to mind. She decided the guy she liked was not going to marry her. So she struck out to another part of the country to attend seminary. That man followed her, waited for her to finish her courses, brought her back home, and married her. He faithfully supported her from afar and visited whenever he could until she got her dreams corralled. The right man will be there at the right time. Sometimes pursuing your dreams can be the impetus that forces him to make a decision!

Personal Confession:

I will set my life in the right order and free myself to live my life to the fullest, whether I have a man or not.

Ruth was doing what was within her power: gleaning and getting what she could out of life. During this exercise, she had plenty of time to gather her thoughts and solidify the issues of her heart. I want to think she communed with God as she silently went about her work and opened herself to new relationships in the midst of a foreign field—all while being totally unaware she was being watched.

Wouldn't you know it? There she is with no makeup on, hair not done, probably not the cutest dress on (a work frock, in fact), and Boaz notices her. He wants to know who she is! Ladies, we spend all of our time doodying ourselves up, and the one day we have not got it together is the day some man decides we are cute. Are we doing all this work for ourselves, for other women, or for members of the opposite sex? Who can say? But when it is your day, no matter how you are looking, it will be your day. Rumor has it that Ruth was an exotic beauty, dark and probably naturally stunning without enhancement. We will never know what really caught Boaz's eye. But, whatever it was, we know he liked what he saw!

Man Fact:
Men are attracted to women who are not looking for a man. They can smell desperation a mile away, and it is sure to make them run in the other direction.

Boaz asked the other workers who she was. Now this is crucial. First, you never know who is watching you. Next, you want to make sure that people are saying the right things about you. What type of reputation are you cultivating? I have a friend who is in ministry. He travels extensively. On one of his ministry trips, he saw a woman in the audience that piqued his interest.

When he inquired about her, he was told she was inconsistent in her walk with God and not a recommendation for him. On that note, he dropped the idea of pursuing her. She missed out on a wonderful man and did not even know it. I have watched men long enough to know how they assess women who cross their path. They are meticulous in their evaluations of the woman's character and other traits long after their interest has been sparked by her appearance. Based on what they conclude, no matter how beautiful she is, they might still pass.

What does your life say about you? Are you happy and whole, or are you miserable and laden down with all sorts of emotional baggage? Your attitude will be revealed in the things you say, the air around you, and even in your outward appearance! Depressed people do not take good care of themselves, and it shows. A man might not know the intimate details, but his radar says something is wrong, and he is off and running in the opposite direction. The other determining factor is what other people say about you when he checks your references. Ruth had references she did not even know of. People observing her had a lot to report to Boaz. The way she took care of her mother-in-law and her strong character overrode the fact she was a foreigner who should be an outcast in their eyes.

You might not have it all together. You might have failed and made awful mistakes in the past. What you make of your life today can override all of your past issues and give you new grace that will open the door to walking in favor, acceptance, and love. God will cover your past and give you a new heart, a new life, and new and fruitful relationships. Harvesttime is about being fruitful—gathering the fruit from seeds sown the season before. Ruth arrived right on time and cultivated a good reputation while she focused on reaping what she could out of life.

What are you reaping in your day-to-day life? How are your relationships faring? Now is the time to work on your interaction with people around you and make sure your connections are sound. If you have issues with your father, please deal with them and resolve them before your mate comes along. You do not want him to become the target of all your unresolved stuff. Get counseling, confront your father, and do whatever is necessary to become healthy in this area. Perhaps he was not around and you live with abandonment issues. Settle these things in your heart. God is the only

Personal Confession:

I will plant only what I want to reap in my life. I will understand that God has given me control over my affairs. When I partner with Him and walk in obedience to His Word, I will reap a fruitful harvest.

perfect Father. Humans are guaranteed to fail. Do not hold them to a standard that is impossible to keep. Everyone deals from the deck he or she has been given. Whatever your personal experiences, you are either paralyzed or empowered by them. Learn to look beyond the faults of people and see their needs. Work on your standing relationships and resolve outstanding matters. Keep short accounts and keep your heart healthy.

Attitude is everything when you approach life. People are watching. They are taking note. Are you happy? Can you hold steady even when life happens and you are hit in a crosswind? How do you deal with crisis and success? Do you change like the wind? Are you moody? Do you harbor an attitude of entitlement and get evil when things do not go your way? The reapers noted Ruth's humility when she asked to glean in the fields. She was nice, nonthreatening, and she came with her hands open, grateful for whatever they wanted to offer.

Many times pride and fear of rejection stop us from being approachable. Our invisible shield is up, and people are bouncing off it! Unaware of the negative air we are pumping out, we reinforce our thinking that no one can be trusted and tighten our resolve not to let anyone in. We refuse to be vulnerable. Doesn't that word just make you tremble? We will talk more about that later. The point is this: If we are not open, no one can come in—even those who want to. It is just too much work, and there are too many other easy options. So check your attitude. Ask some friends who will be honest with you what type of signals you send to people who do not know you well, and ask God to help you lower your defenses. You must learn to hide your heart in Him and allow Him to keep it safe while you continue being yourself, releasing the true you who lives within and wants to reach out to people. Remember, those whom you fear will hurt you are also afraid of rejection.

If you have checked your attitude and find no real problems there, but it seems as if no one approaches you and you are wondering what is wrong with you, never fear. I went through this for a season and I thought to myself, *Is there some weird growth on my forehead I do not know about? Does my breath stink? What is wrong with me?* Finally, the quiet knowledge that God had put a hedge around me for a time to deal with just me became apparent. I began to rest in that season and allow Him to complete what He was doing. It was a time of self-examination and growth, of developing gifts I had overlooked, of literally blossoming as a woman! In the end, I was a much finer package to present to someone. In retrospect, I realize I was not ready and would have been a detriment to any man who would have approached me. Take some time to allow God to unpack your baggage and settle your issues. Clear the decks and be open to love and new beginnings.

Learn to be consistent. The next thing her silent observers in the fields made note of was the fact that Ruth was diligent about what she was doing and not given to losing focus. This was a promising trait for a woman to possess. It meant she was not lazy, but resourceful and dedicated to doing what she had to do to make life happen for her and her family. Yes, they watched her from afar and took note of every little thing. If you think women are observant, you better know that men may not say much, but they see a lot. I remember a male friend telling me he did not talk much because the more he listened, the more he learned. They are watching, ladies, taking note of your disposition, the way you dress and carry yourself, your friends, the way you treat people, and how you respond to circumstances that are not favorable. They are taking notes and checking them twice before they ever decide to approach you. Decide what you want them to see and put it into practice. Do not be superficial. Do your internal work so what they see is truly what they want and get.

Living Life on Purpose

A lot of these issues will go away if your attention is focused where it should be: on moving forward. Concentrate on surviving in the present day and setting up a reserve for the future so you are ready for whatever comes or does not come. One of my favorite stories in the Bible is found in Jeremiah when the children of Israel were taken into captivity. As they sat around waiting to be rescued by God, a prophet by the name of Jeremiah was sent to tell them to get busy with the business of living where they were: building homes, farming the land, marrying, and so on. They were to live as if they were never going to leave, because the reality of the situation was that some of them would not be leaving. They were to remain in Babylon for 70 years! They were urged to be realistic about their circumstances and live life to the fullest anyway. He concluded his message by saying that God knew the plans He had for them.

God knows the plans He has for us, too, but He does not always give us the scoop right away. Does that mean we remain inactive until we get what we want, or do we move past survival mode to overcoming? The Israelites did not like where they were, but the question was, Could they trust God and settle down where He had them? The choice to merely exist versus living was up to them until God released them to return to Israel.

Ruth continued to glean in the fields of Boaz through barley season and wheat season. Let's say she was there about two months, perhaps a little longer, between July and September. She probably saw a lot of Boaz. Did she have a thought about a match being made in heaven or in the fields? Probably not. Remember, she knew she was disqualified as mate material because of her heritage. As far as she was concerned, marriage was not in the cards for her. Her focus was solely on the harvest.

Let's talk about this for a moment. What have you been sowing, and what are you harvesting at present? What do you have to offer to a man? You see, Boaz was a man who was harvesting something. He was not in transition, deciding what he wanted to do with his life. He was a man with a plan, and he was working it. He had something to show for himself. The first rule in discerning if your new man is your Boaz is to see what his harvest looks like. If it is all drama—an accumulation of unfruitful relationships and dreams that are nowhere near coming true—he is not ready to be committed to you. He should be in the harvest season of his life and have good fruit to show for it—spiritual fruit, as well as physical fruit. He comes into your life as a confident man because he knows he has something to offer: a safe place to rest your heart and the means to make provision for you.

As women, we should be equally fruitful. Cultivate a rich abundance of the fruit of the spirit: kindness, goodness, patience, gentleness, faith, love, joy, peace, humility, and self-control. But what about the external stuff? How does your savings account look? What does your home look like? Are you a woman who is prepared to be a wife, to make a house a home, and to add to a household the riches of your own assets? Be what you want to attract. If you want a together man, then be a together woman. Now is the time to prepare yourself, to become the best that you can be. Do not do this just for a man, do it for yourself. God has promised man that when he finds a wife, she will be a blessing and will add to his life and not subtract. Represent...and represent well.

Ponder This

- Make a list of the blessings in your life. Are you content with these? How do these fulfill you?

- What things could you be working on right now to improve your quality of life?

- In what ways are you already living a life of purpose and fruitfulness? In what areas can you improve?

Finish your outdoor work and get your fields ready; after that, build your house (Proverbs 24:27).

7
Recognizing the Man of Your Dreams

*Then Boaz said to Ruth, "You will listen, my daughter,
will you not? Do not go to glean in another field, nor go
from here, but stay close by my young women. Let your
eyes be on the field which they reap, and go after them.
Have I not commanded the young men not to touch you?
And when you are thirsty, go to the vessels and drink
from what the young men have drawn."*

RUTH 2:8-9 NKJV

E very woman dreams of her knight in shining armor coming
to carry her away on a white horse. As little girls, we are
groomed to expect it—to sleep sweetly and be awakened by a
gallant prince who will rescue us from all that threatens. Eventually, we grow up and learn these aspirations are the leftover
remnants of fairy tales. Instead, we decide to settle for someone
like Richard Gere in the movie *Pretty Woman*. It seemed like a
reasonable enough dream that some wealthy business tycoon
would find us breathlessly beautiful, fall in love, shower us in
diamonds and beautiful clothing and the most romantic of
experiences. But alas, this, too, is fiction—delicious fiction,
but fiction nonetheless.

Man Fact:
A good man is a good man, whether rich or poor. A good man can be transformed into a man of means with the right woman by his side.

The reality is most men are just good, honest, hardworking folks who live on a budget. The rich live in a world set apart among their own kind, where they can share and exchange their wealth without losing anything. Or, they are so busy making money, they have no time to enjoy life's pleasures.

Consider what you truly want when it comes to a mate. If you want a friend and companion who will have the time to spend with you, then it is time to kill the fantasy and consider a good man who has a harvest to which you can add.

Who is your Boaz? What does he look like? Well, do not let this scare you, but he usually does not look the way you expected him to look. No matter what he looks like on the outside, his heart will look better than you ever dreamed it would. Will God make you fall in love with an ugly person? No, He will not. He cannot and will not make anyone fall in love with someone. This would be usurping your free will. However, He can help you change your priorities. In the end, someone might look a lot different to you through the eyes of love. And good things do come in the most interesting packages....

What appeals to you about a man's outward appearance is subject to change, but there are some inward characteristics that should always be present. These inner traits separate the men from the boys. Some of us definitely have a problem. It is called a broken chooser. We get giddy over a man's smooth rap and miss the fact that the guy does not keep his promises. He is so fine, but his attitude is downright ugly. He knows how to work women, but he does not like them very much. He is not as mindful of a woman's heart as he should be. (Hmm, am I crunching any toes yet?) He loves himself so much that there is no room in his heart for you. He is into the conquest, but not the commitment. These types of men are not for you.

What type of man is? Let me begin by saying that, from Hollywood stars to major players to the everyday man, one thing is resoundingly the same: When they meet you, they know they want to be with you right away. Every man I have ever inter-viewed said he knew when he met his wife.

Man Fact:
A man knows what he wants when he sees it.

He waited to make sure, and then clinched the deal. This means that a woman must be discerning and look for the signs right away so she does not waste her time or her heart on someone who does not have good intentions toward her.

The Heart of a Man

Check for the Boaz signs. In my book *Secrets of an Irresistible Woman*, I share the three F's you need to gather while dating: fit, fabric, and finance. You also need to look for the four P's: position, pursuit, provision, and protection. Let's break these down one by one. What is this man's position? What is his standing in life and with people around him? Is he making a living? Is he harvesting a good return from the gifts he has sown? Does he even know what his gifts are? A man who has not cultivated this area of his life is restless and finds it hard to settle down because he is still searching for the main part of his identity. He knows he is not ready to offer anything stable or to shoulder the responsibility of another person. Until then, he usually drifts in his relationships with women, staying in one relationship long enough to enjoy the benefits of it, but moving on when he feels the pressure to commit himself on a deeper level.

How do other people view him? Boaz was well-respected and loved by not only his family, but also by his employees and those in high standing in the community. Does the man in your life have long-standing, committed relationships with his friends and associates? What about his friends? Do you like them? Know that he acts just like his friends when he is not around you. What do his coworkers or employees say about him? Do they speak highly of him and commend his character and integrity? Or do they make jokes about his shortcomings? This is a big give-away. Is his family life filled with drama and misunderstanding, or does he walk in harmony with his siblings and parents, especially his mother? A man who loves his mother is an excellent prospect for a husband. Some of these things will take time to find out, but keep them in mind.

Man Fact:
The relationship a man has with his mother and sisters is the same type of relationship he will have with you.

Now, on to the pursuit. After inquiring about Ruth, Boaz then approached her. She did not approach him. I know popular-day date-ology says men like women who have the confidence to approach them. Why? Because men have a greater fear of rejection than we do. However, they are also programmed to pursue, so this can be a delicate matter. The truth, after a bit of prying, is that they like to make the advance but would also appreciate a sign from the woman that the coast is clear to do so.

Positive signs you could send a man would be in the form of your body language. A pleasant smile and eye contact is plenty—just enough to let him know you noticed him, too, and are interested. Then, let him do his thing. Do

Man Fact:
A man knows he is supposed to do the pursuing. When that process is thwarted by a woman's aggressiveness, he will become passive, leaving her to carry the relationship...if it gets that far.

not be so uptight when he approaches. Relax and enjoy the conversation. Remember, you are a fabulous jewel. Believe it and sparkle. Be interested in him and do not bowl him over with too much information about yourself. Listen, be observant, check him out. That first conversation will tell you a lot about him. Is he short on words, but sweet? Then he probably is shy and has good intentions. Is he a little too sure of himself and has all the right lines? Watch this one a little closer and make no emotional investment. After exchanging numbers, how long does it take him to call? If it takes weeks, he has unfinished business elsewhere. Listen to his excuse and see if it rings true to you, but be careful. The average man who is really interested will call within two to three days to see if he can arrange a time for you to get together.

I wouldn't call this a date yet, because nothing has been carved in stone. There have been no promises—nothing is guaranteed. This is what they call in the modeling world a "go-see." You are going out to see if you like one another, that is all. You have way too much data to collect before you even decide if you like him. What you see is not necessarily what you get, so leave your heart at home. Now is not the time to give it away.

The Mating Dance

Even after your first outing, there is a lot that needs to be proven before you can get excited, like if he will call again. What is the next-most-famous men's line right after "Let's just be friends"? You got it: "I'll call you." Sometimes men do not know what to say at the end of the evening, so they just say this line that all women love to hear. It is an easy out.

Personal Confession:

I will make no instantaneous decisions or allow my emotions to run ahead of my mind. I will take the necessary time to assess the man and see if he is worthy of my consideration for a lifetime commitment.

Hearing from him again has everything to do with how he felt about your time together. Did you leave him wanting to get to know you better? This means you left all of your deep, dark secrets in the closet and just had a good time, hopefully finding out more about him than what you were tempted to tell him about yourself. No man on the first encounter wants to hear about past relationships and all that you have been through. Keep it light and have a good time. Pretend you are on "Oprah." What would Oprah ask him about himself? For now, you get to be the interviewer that makes him feel as if he is the star. Remember, men have fragile egos. The more interest you show, the more he will warm up, reveal himself, and also become more curious about you.

Now is not the time to get all deep and spiritual. Did someone gasp? I am just keeping it real! You should *be* spiritual and not have to prove you *are* spiritual by what you say. Jesus had general conversations with people. He opened the door for deeper conversation, but He allowed those He spoke with to choose when they were ready to go beyond where they were. For now, this man just wants to accumulate basic information about you. Are you nice? Do you have a sense of humor? What do you do? What are your interests? Do you like him? That's it. There will be plenty of time for all the important stuff later. Who he is spiritually will be revealed through his conversation, how he handles himself, and how he respects you on your evening out.

Should you hear from him again, and your interaction becomes more regular, you will know you hit the jackpot if he wants to see you on the weekend. This will also let you know if he has someone else in his life or not. A man does not give up the weekends for just anybody. Beware of a man who does not give you his phone number. If there is nothing to hide, he will be transparent with you and give you access to himself, although you should use it sparingly. You are permitted to call once to say you enjoyed yourself with him the day before, just so he knows he is appreciated. Allow him the room he needs to pursue. Men

Personal Confession:

I will not allow my imagination and desires to overrule the reality of where I stand in a man's eyes. I will use my head, as well as my heart, and guard my affections until I know they can be released.

do not like women calling them all the time because it usurps their position in the game. Got it? If he is interested, he will do the pursuing.

A man will do what he has to do to get what he wants. He is not shy or getting over a past relationship when you do not hear from him—he is just not interested. He might be slightly interested, but not enough to do what needs to be done. This would be the case if he has other options, or is aware he really has nothing to offer you. Smart women use their heads as well as their hearts in love. They do not take things personally. If a man cannot see your value and match it, then he is not ready for you. It is best to find this out early in the dance before you invest your heart just because the music sounded good.

Let's move on to the next phase: provision. This is big. There is something about the heart of a man, or should I say the heart of a *real* man, where he wants to make life better for you. He seeks to be the answer to your prayers. As I always say, a man does not want to be your oxygen (unless he is unhealthy), but he does want to be your hero. His heart will be moved to provide for your needs, from physical help to financial help, if need be. This brings up our favorite subject again: vulnerability. Ladies, I know that we "sistahs are doing it for themselves," but can we leave a little somethin' for the men to do for us? A man needs to feel needed. It is marvelous you know how to fix your own car. Just do not do it when he is around. You better learn how to ask for some help! Watch his entire persona change when he feels he has come to your rescue.

Man Fact:
A man wants to know there is a place for him in your world—that he is needed and not merely a decoration.

The Ways of a Woman

Women have become self-sufficient in so many ways, partly out of necessity and partly out of frustration, that they often cannot depend on anyone other than themselves. But this does not have to be the case. Most men have abdicated being gallant because they no longer feel needed. In the midst of their own frustration at being robbed of what proves them to be men, their reaction is, "Fine! Do it yourself, then."

Though we are running corporations and "moving and shaking" out there in the marketplace, be careful. Do not sacrifice your femininity before you consider all that it will cost you. A woman behaving like a man will walk a lonely path because she leads men to assume they are not needed. This does not mean you should flip to the opposite extreme and reveal all your woes. This is overwhelming to a man. Besides, he can only solve one problem at a time. Most men are not multitaskers, so only give out as much information as they can do something about at the present. Table all talk about past relationship dramas and ex-boyfriends. Some wounds you have to allow God to heal, then move on. Do not make other people responsible for past pain and disappointment. Nor do you want him to ponder your contribution to your past.

When Boaz approached Ruth, she did not go into a long dirge about all the hardships she had endured. He had already spotted her present need and addressed it by making provision for her. Not only did he instruct his workers to drop extra grain for her to gather, he also reiterated that no one was to trouble her. Her welfare was uppermost in his mind. He then told her not to glean in anyone else's field. She was to remain in his until the harvest was completed. She thanked him for his consideration, smiled, and went back to what she was doing.

This brings me to my next point: protection. The heart of a Boaz kind of man will not lead you on. He will be an intentional man and keep his accounts short with you. If he is not looking for a relationship, he will say so. If he wants a relationship, he will let it be known. If the man in your life does not tell you to not glean in any other field, take note. Do not establish a relationship in your mind that does not exist. If you have been seeing this man for some time and he has never brought up the subject of his intentions, you can ask him how he feels about your relationship. Where does he see it going? You have been having a wonderful time with him and just wanted

> **Man Fact:**
> A man needs to know you are interested, but he wants to decide the course of the relationship.

to know how he was feeling about the time you shared together. Leave the door open for him to step through. Do not demand a commitment or give ultimatums! This never turns out the way you want it to.

Ruth minded her own business, stayed focused on what she had come to do, and allowed Boaz to make the overtures toward her. At mealtime, he invited her to eat beside him, literally passing food to her to eat. He stayed close to show his position and his care for her. I am sure the other reapers lifted an eyebrow to one another when he left. I can imagine the conversation: "Hmm! Well, could it be that Boaz sees something he likes? He's never told us to drop extra grain for the gleaners before! A little possessive, don't you think, telling us not to bother her or rebuke her for taking more than her share? Oh, yes, I would say that someone has finally caught the eye of our boss."

Your Boaz's provision for you will be evident to other people and they will know you are not just any woman. You are special. There will be a change in the attitude of his friends toward you—a quiet respect. You have become the *one* that should be treated differently from the rest. When a man switches into commitment mode, you will know it.

How do you know his heart is not there? When he is not moved to be a part of your world. If he never wants to go any deeper in conversation and sticks close to the surface, he is just out for a pleasant time, nothing more. If he never wants to expose you to his friends or family, that is an even bigger red flag. If he wants to avoid your friends and family, he is avoiding raising any expectations in your heart and their minds about where he stands with you. If he is only skimming the surface in relating to you, even though he offers help when he sees a need you have, let him go. His body may be beside you, but his mind is on the other side of town, as the song goes. Staying clear and realistic will preserve your heart and keep you from wasting time. One big tip: If you are ready to be married, do not date men who are not interested in marriage or marriage material. You have better things to do with your heart and your time.

It has been said that if you have to ask the price, you cannot afford it. The same is true with love. If you have to play with daisies to determine if he cares for you, you already know the answer. When a man is serious about you, he will make sure you know it because he will want the rules of the game to change from a free-for-all to an exclusive match. The only time this might get iffy is if you are sending mixed signals that set him off-kilter. In this scenario, he might take flight rather than risk the pain of rejection, so be real. Stay open to where he wants the relationship to go. Give him the chance to grow comfortable with his feelings for you so he feels safe to declare what is in his heart. Love is not the arena for playing games. Remain transparent. Ruth was transparent in her humility and thankfulness to Boaz. She was truly appreciative of his kindness and attention to her, a foreigner. This only drove him to reassure her that he was indeed serious about his commitment to take care of her.

This goes to prove my final point. There was nothing Ruth could do for Boaz really. She did not have any money. She could not buy him gifts. She did not have a telephone, so she could not call him in case he was shy. All she

Personal Confession:

I will resist the urge to perform in order to win love. I will trust love to come to me.

could do was be herself. She could not even fancy herself up. All she could do was be appreciative of him, and that was enough. She left him in the position of power, and he did not abuse it. She allowed him to feel like a man. I believe we are all looking for a real man. This means we have to allow a man to just be. She was a woman, soft but strong, warm, caring, and humble. No airs or pretenses, she was simply Ruth, and he loved her for it. Why not give it a try and simply be you?

Ponder This

- What type of men have you allowed yourself to settle for in the past? Were they truly what you wanted or deserved?

- How do your insecurities cause you to settle for men who are not worthy of your heart?

- What qualities have you looked for in the past in a man? In what ways has your emphasis been wrong?

Many a man claims to have unfailing love, but a faithful man who can find? (Proverbs 20:6).

8

Turning the Tide

*Then Naomi her mother-in-law said to her, "My daughter,
shall I not seek security for you, that it may be well with
you? Now Boaz...is winnowing barley tonight at the
threshing floor. Therefore wash yourself and anoint yourself,
put on your best garment and go down to the threshing floor;
but do not make yourself known to the man until he has
finished eating and drinking. Then it shall be, when he lies
down, that you shall notice the place where he lies; and you
shall go in, uncover his feet, and lie down; and he will tell
you what you should do."*

RUTH 3:1-4 NKJV

This chapter is loaded with goodies, so we will go through it
carefully. When it is time to close the deal, a lot weighs in the
balance. It pays to make the right moves. The first thing to
master in a relationship is being sensitive to the right time. Every
season has signs to let you know when it is coming to a close. In
spring, it stays light longer; in the fall, the leaves turn on the
trees and eventually fall off; in winter, it gets dark earlier. In the
cycle of love, the more he cares, the more he will want to be
with you, and he will stay longer. He will begin to purge his little
black book—letting other people know he is now "involved"

with someone. All the deadweight and fillers in his life will be removed to make more room for time with you.

When love is in bloom, you must be mindful of the signs so you will be ready for what comes next. This, of course, will not be totally left up to you. You must stay sensitive spiritually and keep close to the heart of God. God will always let you know what time it is. In Ruth's situation, it was Naomi who decided what should happen next. You might say, in a way, Naomi could be an illustration of how the Holy Spirit works in our lives. When God decides it is time for something to happen, He will, through His Spirit, instruct you in the way you should go.

You can decide it is time for you to get married, but if that is not what God has in mind for you at the time, it will not happen. I have known several women who have loudly proclaimed they had written on their calendars that they were going to be married by the end of the year. Well, the end of the year came and went with no marriage, and then they had issues with God. The best approach is to seek and find out what God has in mind for you before proclaiming what you are going to do. "In his heart a man plans his course, but the LORD determines his steps" (Proverbs 16:9). When God decides it is time for something to take place in your life, watch out—nothing can stop it from coming to pass!

Remember, way back in the garden of Eden, God decided it was time for Adam to have a mate. Adam never brought it up. God decided one day that it would be better for Adam to have help in carrying out his assignment in the garden. He caused Adam to fall into a deep sleep and created a helpmeet for him— someone who was shaped and molded to exactly fit into Adam's needs. She would be the missing part of him—made from him and for him, a helper specially equipped to assist him in his assignment. They would complement one another perfectly because they were a part of each other. This was God's plan and design for marriage. Two people become one because, in their spirits, they are joined in common vision and passion.

When God chooses the time, He will also do the mate selection (that is, if we allow Him to). Naomi selected the time and the mate. She decided it was time for Ruth to have stability and security in her life. They could not live off her gleaning forever.

Though this is not a topic Ruth brought up, it was decided that yes, indeed, it was time to take her life to the next level. Notice the reasoning behind why Naomi decided it was time for Ruth to be married: to ensure her future security.

Personal Confession:

I will trust God with the timing of delivering my heart's desires, according to His knowledge of my needs.

When God decides you need someone in order to live through the next season of your life more effectively, He will set things in motion. He decided Adam needed help, and Naomi decided Ruth needed help. I often tell singles, "You do not need help doing nothing. Get busy doing what you were created to do, and that will propel you into position to meet your life partner." God creates teams. He created the animals two by two. Jesus sent the disciples out two by two. King Solomon said that two were better than one because they would have a good return for their labor. Teamwork gets things done. No man or woman is an island. One cannot bear fruit alone. It takes two, planting seeds together, to get a mutual harvest.

Completing the Harvest

In order to move to the next level of life, you must complete your assignment for the season you are in. How will you know when it is complete? You will not know until God says so. If you are applying yourself to life in the right manner, you actually will not care because you will be so engrossed in your present mission or project. You will then sense change in the air and know something new is happening, although you do not know exactly what. You will feel a sense of conclusion and mission accomplished. The season will change in your heart first. God will begin to condition it to receive the next phase of your life. When Adam awoke to find Eve standing there, he knew who she was and why she was there. He named her and embraced her. This is why it is so important that the season in the man's and woman's life has had the time to be completed and bear fruit. There will be no guessing games. The man will know who you are and be ready for you.

Naomi also decided Boaz was the perfect match because he was family. He was from her own people. Oneness and being a part of each other has a lot to do with the similarities of the partners. Small wonder God created the animals after "like kind." Though opposites often attract, it is the similarities that keep couples together. Things they agree on build bridges that they can cross to their dreams. A house divided will fall. The more you have in common, the better.

Personal Confession:

I will be cognizant of the seasons of my life and sensitive to the times. I will not lag behind or try to run ahead. I will practice resting and thriving in the season I am in.

Naomi expertly noted it was the end of the harvest season. It was time. Ruth could not go any further in her gleaning. The fields were stripped bare. Boaz had harvested all that he could and had a great return for his labor. Naomi knew this was perfect timing. Boaz was not in a season of lack, and there would be no hesitation, no questions of how he could provide for Ruth. The evidence stood clearly before him. He would be in good humor because he had realized a rich return for his investment and hard work. A man knows what his duties are, and he also knows if he is equipped to fulfill them. Listen to his conversation. When he says, "I don't deserve you," believe him. If he says, "I am not ready for a commitment," again, believe him!

Contrary to popular belief, a woman does *not* fix a man or change his mind. When a man senses that a woman is

Man Fact:
If he does not bring up the subject of commitment, he does not want one.

trying to fix him, he becomes obstinate and uncooperative. He takes what you do not like about him to the extreme, or he moves on in search of someone who will accept him the way he is. Men do not like to be "fixed." And neither do we, so that is fair. A woman can definitely be a positive influence on a man's life once he is committed to her, but a man has to fix himself with the help of God. Because of his love for you, he becomes motivated to be the best man he can be for you, but he will never respond to a demand for change.

A Season of Change

There comes a time in a man's life when he becomes aware of the fact that he needs a wife in order to get to the next level of life. This is when mating season begins. Until then, it is open season. He is open to dating all women who are available to

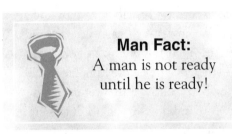

Man Fact:
A man is not ready
until he is ready!

him. He feels no sense of urgency to commit yet, because he is not in the season for marrying. Sometimes you will meet a man you feel is perfect for you. He has all of the qualities you desire, but he is simply not ready to give you his heart. It is possible to meet the right person at the wrong time. Be able to discern your season and let him go. Who knows, perhaps he will return at a later date. Do not grieve over passing up "the right man." The "right person" at the wrong time can be more painful than dealing with the wrong person at any time!

The Perfect Soul Mate

There is also the issue of what we call a "soul mate." Let me clear this up for you. There is usually in the life of every woman an encounter with someone who seems to fit so perfectly that it is almost like being with herself. But it seems this is the person who does not remain. For the rest of our days, we think back on him with fond remembrances and wonder if we will ever meet another man like that, another "soul mate." I heard a preacher say once that you do not need someone just like you because if both of you were alike, one of you would be unnecessary! Good point, but consider another. If you are both alike, then you have the same weaknesses. There will be no one in the mix to balance you out. This could be a problem if you are not good with finances, or details, or a host of other things that make life run smoothly. So you had an encounter with someone who actually did nothing to promote growth in your life, but you were simply happy, happy, happy! You had good chemistry, good times, good everything. That is not how real life goes, is it?

Internalize this for a moment. God is your Soul Mate. From the moment He breathed the breath of life into your being and you became a living soul, your spirit naturally longed to be held in an eternal kiss with its Creator. This longing for an unbroken connection to satisfy us is rooted in our desire to be joined to God. Once we realize this, we can know we have already found our Soul Mate. We must have the patience to wait for a companion handpicked by God to not only help us, but also to stretch us and bring out the best in us.

Taking Care of Self

Naomi was a wise woman. She waited until just the right time and then instructed Ruth on how to make her move. Naomi proceeded practically in the instructions she gave. She knew that no matter how good a man is, you have to please his eyes and senses before you can capture his heart. She was not concerned with Ruth's appearance until it was time to take her relationship with Boaz to another level. Boaz had seen Ruth only in work mode. Perhaps her hair was tucked under a scarf to protect it from the sun and dust in the fields. Standing, bending, stretching, and lifting was natural exercise that probably had her pretty toned after several months. The sun had deepened her already olive complexion. I am sure she was an exotic sight to behold—a natural beauty. Obviously, she had caught his eye in the first place. Out of all of the workers and gleaners in the field, she was the one who stood out in the crowd. However, he had not ever seen her in her full glory when she was all done up, if you know what I mean. Naomi decided Boaz needed to see Ruth at her best in order to clinch the deal (even though it was his familial obligation to marry Ruth). I will explain more about this a little later.

Now let's focus on you. How do you feel about your appearance? We have dealt with your inner qualities a lot, but now it is time to deal with the outside—the first glimpse of you that anyone sees. In order to get that man to come your way, he has got to like what he sees. Let's get real. When a man walks into the room, it is not his spirit that turns our heads in his direction. It is his outward appearance. We do not turn to a girlfriend and say, "Oh, what a nice heart he has!" No! We say, "My, my, now that's a fine brother there!"

We take note of his height, weight, grooming, clothing, and the way he carries himself. Does he have a nice smile, great eyes, nice hands, good shoes? We take stock of that man from head to toe, and then decide we want to get more information. On the flip side of this equation, a bold brother, who might not be as fine, can still win our hearts if he has a good rap. Women do tend to be moved more by what they hear, even though looks can be an initial motivator. Men, on the other hand, are moved first by what they see. So it would behoove us to always put our best foot forward.

Taking care of yourself is the best investment you can make in yourself. You can be the most wonderful person in the world, but a man will never find that out if there is not something about you that grabs his attention. That does not mean you have to dress like the women in the videos we see on MTV. What it does mean is you need to take the time to nurture your body. Everyone is not going to have six-pack abs, but some sort of exercise is crucial to your well-being, even walking. It helps your posture, your heart, your energy level, and your skin. Your overall body profits from exercise. You will feel better about you when your body feels good. Many women are suffering from fatigue because they have not released enough energy to create energy in their bodies. Do not focus on being a supermodel; just focus on being fit and healthy. Men will tell you they are not set on having a woman who is a size 2, but they do find a woman very attractive, no matter what size, if she is happy with herself and confident in the skin she has.

Examine your eating habits. Has food become your sanctuary during your singleness? This is one sanctuary that can turn into a lonely prison if you continue to seek solace there. Do not beat yourself up about where you are physically. Just begin to lovingly get your body back on track. For years, I struggled with my weight until recently. I gave my body back to God and decided to finally allow Him to lead me to a place of victory. The first thing I had to accept was I could no longer eat anything I wanted. When I graduated from high school, I weighed 103 pounds with clothes on! Over the years, my weight has escalated as high as 185 pounds. I had three different sizes in my wardrobe. As my weight seesawed up and down, I discovered new outfits in my own closet. Tired of the up and down, I finally threw up my hands and asked God for help.

The Body Beautiful

The first thing I did was a cleansing program for 21 days to free my system from all the junk and toxins it was holding onto. The program included seven days of fasting and drinking tons of water and a little bit of fruit juice or herbal tea, one week of fruit only, and the third week adding in vegetables. I was so encouraged by the change in my body in just this short period, it spurred me to go on. I then read books on eating according to my blood type. Incorporating this information with what I had gleaned about food combining, I proceeded to make a lifestyle change. I was finished with dieting. I was going to listen to my body and follow its directions. Anytime I was tempted to eat something I was not supposed to, I imagined someone pouring poison on top of it, and that was enough to keep me on the straight path! I have now accepted the fact that if I want to feel and look good, I have to be good to myself and not abuse my body. Emotional eating only spurs more emotional eating and can be a deceptive cycle if you do not nip it in the bud.

Personal Confession:

I will purpose to be kind to my body, to nurture it, and love it. I will make the investment of keeping my temple in the best condition for God's glory, as well as my own well-being.

I encourage you to take the time to find out what works for your body and be kind to yourself. Remember, you have to like yourself first before anyone else will. The ugly alternative is to get caught up in a cycle of abusive relationships because your own self-hatred has convinced you that is all you deserve. But this is not true, according to God. No matter what condition you are in, He is consistent with His love and protection over you. A man should never treat you as less valuable than the Most High would. Use God's love and compassion as your gauge.

Getting Beyond Skin Deep

Now what about your skin? What you put in your body affects your skin, as well as what you put on it. Take advantage of the free consultations at department stores to find out what works best to create a more beautiful you. Use products when cleansing your face and body that will moisturize and hydrate your skin from your face to your toes. We spend so much money on clothing to cover up the body, and yet ignore the body itself. The foundation of any building dictates the condition of anything that is added to it. Begin to invest in your body, and your body will give you its best by looking good and functioning well. Of course, the best beauty secret for skin is lots of water. It flushes out toxins and give you a natural glow.

Try to find a subtle, but complimentary fragrance for yourself. Every woman should have a signature fragrance—one that leaves something on a man's mind. It should be so distinctly you that if he smells it anywhere else, his thoughts should turn to you. I usually select a fragrance according to the seasons. When it is summer, I choose a lighter fragrance—a soft floral with vanilla undertones. For winter, I choose one that is a little heavier like musk and amber—perfect for when it is cold outside because it smells warm. I do not jump back and forth every other day wearing different fragrances. I stick to one, and that scent identifies me. Select a fragrance that warms to your skin. You will need to spray it on and allow it a few minutes to dry to see how it mixes with your body chemistry. If you like what you smell and feel it reflects your personality, then go for it! Fragrance has to be important if the Bible took the time to tell us that Queen Esther spent 12 months being prepared to meet the king by having her diet changed, soaking in special baths, and being anointed with various oils. There is something to this. These are some of the delightful arts of womanhood. Indulge yourself. Naomi told Ruth to wash herself and anoint herself. She wanted her to smell pretty and be pretty when she presented herself to Boaz.

Dressing for the Part

Next on Ruth's instruction list was to put on her best garment. Naomi wanted Ruth to put her best face forward by washing herself, perfuming herself with exotic oils, and finally, dressing in a manner that would be appealing to Boaz. Let's talk about this for a minute. Contrary to popular opinion and what the media sells, a man does not like everything hanging out on the woman he wants to take home to present to his mother. As I point out in my book *The Unspoken Rules of Love* (WaterBrook Press, 2003), men categorize women into three groups: the friend, the freak, and the forever. How you present yourself is one of the first factors that determines where you land in a man's mind. First impressions are lasting ones. Lots of women dress to get a man's attention, and then become insulted when they get the wrong type of attention. This should tell you that a man has a different idea of what is attractive. What you wear makes you someone he takes seriously or as a plaything. There is definitely a difference between attraction and respect. You can be attracted to someone that you do not respect. The goal is to have both in operation.

An air of mystery will leave more on his mind than if you leave nothing to his imagination. When a book gives away the ending on the back cover, there is no longer any need or urgency to buy the book. The story has already been told. It kind of takes the fun out of it, don't you think? A man wants the woman in his life to be his secret garden. Buy clothing that compliments you without revealing too much. This does not mean you should shroud and hide yourself, but accentuate your positives in good taste. Be appealing, not overwhelming. Accept a man's attention graciously when he gives it and move on, or stop if he invites you to. Please do not get all spiritual when a brother is checking you out and berate him for being carnal. Practicing Christian or not, a man is wired to be appreciative of a woman's beauty. God created him that way.

Man Fact:
Men do make value judgments about women based on how they dress. Select the way you want to be viewed and dress accordingly.

The Waiting Game

After getting all freshened up, Ruth was to wait until Boaz had finished eating and drinking. Then she was to notice where he chose to rest. It is a fact that most women are ready and settled on what they want to happen in a relationship before the man is. However, just because you know what you want does not mean you can force the issue. A man will dig in his heels and deliberate all the more, that is, if he does not just flee. Naomi said, "Let him party and finish his celebration...let him unwind, and then make your move." A man is more responsive when he is relaxed—when he is not worrying about work, about how he is going to tackle this or gain control of that. He usually likes to focus on one thing at a time. This is hard for most women to understand because we are such multitaskers. A man is not a woman, so do not expect him to think, act, or respond like we do. Let him finish what he is doing. Wait until you can have his full attention.

Watch and observe, notice his moods, and learn to gauge when he is relaxed. It is so much easier to get what you want when someone is in a good mood. Nothing irritates a man more than a woman interrupting his groove. It is the quickest way to be dismissed. This is not because he does not care, but because he wants to get back to finishing what he was doing. Remember, until he feels good about himself and knows he really has something to offer and be a real man to you, he will not be able to commit.

Recently, I took a trip to another city. The pilot announced we would get to leave early. Everyone aboard was happy at the thought of reaching their destination sooner than expected. However, when we arrived at the next airport, our gate was occupied and we were forced to wait on the ground anyway. The moral of this story? You will either wait for God to deliver His promises to you, or you will wait for Him to deliver you out of the mess you've gotten yourself into. Either way, you will wait! So trust God's timing and rest in it. He is always on time.

What a Woman's Got to Do

When Ruth reached the threshing-room floor, Boaz was in good spirits after celebrating the conclusion of the harvest. He lay down to go to sleep. Softly, she uncovered his feet, laid down, and pulled the corner of the cover over herself. According to the customs of the day, this was literally a marriage proposal. Whoa! *That was bold*, you may be thinking. Before you get carried away and think you can do the same, let me explain something to you. Ruth had the right to do this according to Jewish tradition. The law in Israel stated that if a woman's husband died, his brother or next of kin was to take her as his wife and sire children so the dead man's inheritance would not be lost and his name would continue. Ruth had a right to ask for his covering.

Proposing to a man these days is not wise because the situation is entirely different. First of all, there is no set custom that encourages this—you would be out there on your own. The Word of God states, "He who finds a wife finds what is good" (Proverbs 18:22). *He!* A real man names his wife, just as Adam did. *He* makes the declaration of *his* intentions. What happens when a woman

Man Fact:
A man knows what he wants when he meets you. His mind is already made up. He merely waits to make sure. If it takes a long time for him to make a decision, it is because he has no intention of ever committing to you.

does the pursuing and actually wins the man? At first he may respond positively because he is flattered, until he sees something *he* really wants to pursue. He will probably leave you and be engaged in a short period of time because he got what he wanted. Many women who have been dating a man for years experience this and are shocked at how quickly this same man committed to someone else.

Men are hunters by nature. Their conquest is not complete if they have not been able to experience the hunt in all of its stages. If you do happen to get the man down the aisle, you will learn something about him quickly after you have said "I do." He will be passive in other areas that are important to you. All of a sudden this realization becomes magnified in your eyes because you thought that once you had convinced him where he needed to be, he would stand up and be the mighty leader and loving cover you wanted in the first place. Sorry, if he is passive in approaching you, he is a passive man—period. The average male has aggressive hormones that propel him into pursuit mode when he sees something he wants.

If you see someone you like, but he isn't interested, enjoy the view and keep stepping. Avoid heartache by not starting something that might not have a great finish. If he did not make a move, he either was not attracted to you in the same way, or he has issues you cannot do anything about. If you do the pursuing, even if you get the man, you will spend the rest of your relationship carrying it or pressing him for validation and assurance that he really wants you. Nothing he does or says will ever be enough to place your heart at rest.

Discerning the Times

Should a woman tell a man she loves him before he tells her? I would not advise it. The *L* word is frightening to them. Men receive that word better from you after they have given it. Feel free to tell how much you enjoy being with him and how wonderful he is, but wait to express deeper feelings until he is ready to receive them. This would be after he has rounded up the courage to deal with his own emotions and finally share them with you. Stay open, stay vulnerable, but use your head and wait for verbal cues to follow. Allow him to be the leader in the relationship, charting its course. Your job is to keep him accountable. You may ask where the relationship is going, but you should never take over the oars unless you feel it is time to get out of the boat.

How do you know when it is time to ask where you are heading? Certainly not after the first three dates! Wait until you notice he is spending more time with you on a regular basis, making more intimate moves toward you, beginning to expose you to family and friends, as well as scheduling things to do together for the future. Do not become readily available if you do not know where you stand in the relationship. Do not behave like a wife unless you are a wife. Remember what Mama told you: "Why buy the cow when you can get the milk for free?" This does not address just sex. It addresses all the other wonderful benefits of marriage as well.

Personal Confession:

I will not be afraid of being vulnerable; rather, I will see the strength in it. I will learn to master the art of submission, availing myself to be blessed by other people as I walk with open hands.

The delicate balance of being available, but not overtly navigating the course of the relationship, must be mastered.

So if you cannot lie down at the feet of your Boaz and ask him to marry you, what can you do? You can be vulnerable, available, and open. You can let the man in your life know that you need him. Remember, a hero lies in the heart of every man. He is drawn not only to your beauty and goodness, but also to your need for him. Not just financially or physically, though he may respond to some of those needs, but the deeper need of his love and commitment to you. The independent "I don't need a man" woman does not make a man secure enough to think he could be her knight in shining armor. Those women who have an "I can take care of myself" attitude usually end up doing just that.

Ruth listened to the wise counsel of Naomi and did as she was told. She humbly submitted herself to Boaz and was honest about what she needed from him. She needed him to be a "kinsman-redeemer," a man who would redeem her life with his own. Isn't this what most women want? If we are truly honest with ourselves and other people, I believe we will find such a man.

- How is your self-esteem? What things can you do to become a better and more confident you?

- Are you getting the response from men that you want? What things do you need to develop or alter in order to change their perception of you?

- What attitudes and fears keep you from being open and vulnerable in emotional situations?

*Your beauty should not come [only] from outward adornment,
such as braided hair and the wearing of gold jewelry and fine
clothes. Instead, it should be that of your inner self,
the unfading beauty of a gentle and quiet spirit,
which is of great worth in God's sight*
(1 Peter 3:3-4).

9
A Woman of Virtue

Then he [Boaz] said, "Blessed are you of the LORD, my daughter!
For you have shown more kindness at the end than at the
beginning, in that you did not go after young men, whether poor or
rich. And now, my daughter, do not fear. I will do for you all that
you request, for all the people of my town know that you are a vir-
tuous woman. Now it is true that I am a close relative; however,
there is a relative closer than I. Stay this night, and in the morning
it shall be that if he will perform the duty of a close relative for
you—good; let him do it. But if he does not want to perform the
duty for you, then I will perform the duty for you....Lie down until
morning." So she lay at his feet until morning and she arose before
one could recognize another. Then he said, "Do not let it be
known that the woman came to the threshing floor."

RUTH 3:10-14 NKJV

Can you conceive of this: Boaz, rich Boaz, actually thought of
it as a privilege that little Miss Ruth, who had nothing to offer
but herself, would want him? (Actually, she did have something
to offer—her husband's family field—but Boaz certainly did not
need it.) He obviously found her beautiful because he seemed to
think she could have her pick of who she wanted. This is a nice
thought, but not exactly realistic because of her heritage. Boaz
had been prepared to embrace Ruth no matter what.

Many women wonder if they really are worthy of getting a good man because of their past mistakes, race, life condition, looks, you name it. We all have reasons for a mounting list of insecurities. I want to set you free right now by telling you this: The man that is for you will not regard your life scars as deterrents. God will shape his heart to accommodate who you are. The things that do not belong there, or that God does not want to subject the man to, He will work with you to change or remove. But as for the things about you that cannot be reversed or changed, He will make room in the heart of your man to look beyond your faults and see your needs.

The reason Boaz could be so open to the thought of marrying Ruth was because he was well-acquainted with what it felt like to be an outcast because of background. His own mother was Rahab, the harlot—the woman who had helped the spies from Israel who came to scope out Jericho before the walls fell down. She married one of those spies by the name of Salmon. Together, they gave birth to Boaz. Yes, Boaz knew a thing or two about being ostracized for things you cannot change. It made him a very gracious man who was open to dealing with people according to who they were as individuals.

God has a man for you no matter what your race, background, and mistakes have been. Stop apologizing for who you are and begin to embrace your own uniqueness. Know that the things you have been through have made you the valuable person and gift you are today. God can use your experiences to benefit other people. Allow Him to use your pain and your past mistakes. Let God squeeze the lessons out of them and make lemonade to pour out and refresh people around you.

Be Open

Talking about Boaz brings up a great point. Perhaps he had not pursued her any further because in his mind he was not her type, maybe a bit too old. What is your "type"? We all have these preconceived notions of what our mate should look like or be like. Yet, most of the happily married women I talk to tell me the same thing about their husbands: He was not what she had in mind, but she sure is glad she got him. He turned out to be better than what she had imagined for herself. I also find that, as a woman gets older, she begins to relax a bit and release preconceived notions. The list of things he must be grows shorter. Maybe she becomes more in tune with what is truly important. Perhaps she is just more realistic. Whatever the reason, surface stuff that has nothing to do with the man himself falls by the wayside. Issues such as height, hair, coloring, muscles, exotic background, and even massive wealth become unimportant—as they should. We will delve into this a little deeper later.

Men are basically insecure beings, no matter how desirable they are. They fear rejection big time. We know Boaz was no slouch. He was wealthy, respected, and kind. We do not know what he looked like, but he was probably very handsome. King David was his great grandson, and it was said he was extremely handsome.

Man Fact:
The average man fears rejection from the woman in whom he is interested. He needs permission to approach you (unless he is bold or crazy). A smile, eye contact, something subtle but direct, is enough to give him a cue.

Good looks probably ran in the family. What was considered older back in those days is not what older is today. Older could have been 40, for all we know, which is still young if you take care of yourself. From all indications, he probably did. And yet, we find him being flattered that Ruth would consider him.

Boaz then notes there is an obstacle to him being able to offer her his hand in marriage. I wonder if this was why he had not voiced an interest in her in the first place. There was another relative in line for her hand before him, who was closer in kin than he was. But he would handle the matter! I like a man who takes control, rises to the occasion, and solves the problem. He explained that if the closer relative did not want to do his duty by her, he would. I really like that—a man of principle! He advised her to lie down and sleep until the morning—in other words, to not worry her pretty little head about a thing. She could rest in the knowledge that her request was already a done deal. Don't you just love a man who can keep his promises? Money isn't everything, but a man who keeps his word is.

Ruth did as Boaz instructed her. She lay at his feet until morning. Now you *know* we have to talk about this! You knew we were not going to get out of this book without bringing up the S word: sex. She lay at his feet until morning. Nothing happened! As a matter of fact, he woke her up early and sent her on her way because he did not want anyone to see her and begin gossiping about what had not occurred. He became guardian of her reputation, safety, and well-being.

The "S" Word

When a man really cares about you, he will care about all of you—including your spiritual and emotional health. He will not want to compromise you in any way or violate anything that is important to you. Believe it or not, even a man in the secular world will put off having sex with you to preserve your special-ness in his eyes if he thinks you might be "The One." A man does not like to have the thought you had sex with someone before him. Subcon-sciously, he still desires a virgin. To a man, a sex life in your past means you found other men just as special as he is. Will he be better or worse than your last experience? Will you compare him to other men? His identity is deeply rooted in his sexual performance and your response to him.

> **Man Fact:**
> Though they will push you, men are disappointed if you give in. They want to know they are desirable to you, but that you have self-control. Otherwise, the thought in the back of their minds is, "Is she this easy with every guy?" Yes, my sisters, when it comes to sex, men have double standards.

I find most women do not stand on principle when it comes to sex because they do not understand the depths of what sex is really all about. For everything in the spiritual realm, there is a natural parallel. Sex could be considered a natural parallel to the spiritual act of worship. What is sex? What is worship? It is giving all you have and all you are to the one you love. It is com-pletely yielding yourself to your lover, submitting to him, praising him. Deep, isn't it? Small wonder those people who wor-shiped idols always included sexual orgies as part of their rituals. Even the heathen understood the spiritual implications of sex.

This is why God considers sex outside of marriage, or forni-cation, to be adultery. He feels we are taking worship away from Him and giving it to an idol. If someone has been elevated to such a place in our heart that we would disobey God, then truly that man has become an idol. God is not into sharing His women until He turns them over to the one whom He has chosen to be the physical extension of His love toward them.

Sex was intended by God to bind two people together. Have you ever noticed, for those of you who are not virgins, that it is harder to break off a relationship with someone you have slept with? Do you know why? There are several reasons. The first reason is because sex goes beyond the physical act to the spiritual. You actually create a soul tie with the other person. You are literally fused to that person. To separate now becomes a painful ordeal. It is literally a stripping of the soul, like a scarred tree that continues to grow but is marked for life. Long after the separation, phantom pain remains. Even if you had concluded you did not even like the person, something within you longs for him. Some women are convinced the only way to put out the fire of longing is to return to the same bad situation time and time again. The only thing that happens is the tie grows stronger. A decision must be made to end the relationship once and for all, while trusting time and the Spirit of God to eventually ease your torment.

Secondly, there is a shame element to breaking up. In most translations, when the Bible speaks of someone having God-ordained sex, the word *know* is used. "And Adam knew Eve…and she conceived" (Genesis 4:1 KJV). Whenever it was a union outside of God's perfect design, the Bible says "and he *lie* with her" (a good choice of words), or "he *went unto* her." This knowing spoke of deep intimacy—of someone knowing you in a way that no one else did, of being naked and unashamed, of being completely transparent and hiding nothing from the one you love. Now consider the breakup. This man walks away carrying pieces of yourself that you will never recover—your secrets, the very essence of who you are. He can no longer be trusted to guard your heart. What will he do with this delicate information? Will he pass it on to other people or, will he do worse and simply despise you? This is the worst type of rejection. It is irreconcilable to the human spirit. Your soul was not designed to be subjected to such a tearing. It was designed for eternal relationships. Small wonder it takes such a toll on your heart and emotions. No one is supposed to "know" you that well except for your husband. The one who will remain and guard the innermost parts of you.

Personal Confession:

I will not subject my heart or my spirit to such a damaging circumstance by giving myself to someone before marriage. I will purpose to keep my body for my wedding night and will not compromise before then.

Next, after putting yourself in the position to literally worship a man, come the other possibilities to which you open yourself: STD's (sexually transmitted diseases). Every woman always thinks it would never happen to her, yet it surprises every victim. It is probably Murphy's favorite law. Then there is the other life-long consequence: pregnancy. Suddenly your life has been altered for the rest of your days. Your destiny has taken a sudden turn you did not anticipate. Sacrifices and changes you had not planned to make are now necessary. Life, as you knew it, will be over. Your freedom, so sorely taken for granted, will be gone forever. This is not just a new chapter in your life; it is a whole new book. Though children are a blessing, they are also hard work, and single-parenting is a lonely and exhausting job.

Alternative Measures

Now I hear someone asking, "Well, Michelle, what do I do with my needs? I am suffering! I don't know if I can hold out any longer! If I'm not supposed to have sex, why won't God take the desire away from me?" God is not going to do that because He gave you the desire in the first place. Yes, it is a healthy, God-given desire. You must learn to master your desires. What would happen if you ate whatever you wanted, whenever you felt like it? You would blow up! Everything that feels good *to* you may not be good *for* you. There is a time and place for everything. Your attitude toward yourself, as well as your view of what sex is truly all about, must change in order for you to prioritize your standards and keep from walking around like a deprived victim, bereft of joy and fulfillment.

Man Fact:

A man, generally speaking, is resentful of a woman when she gets pregnant before marriage. He feels manipulated and trapped by her. He will rebel against being forced to commit to a woman to whom he did not choose to commit. His way of maintaining control is to abdicate responsibility for the child and sever the relationship with the woman.

"What about oral sex and masturbation?" you may ask. These two areas I get questioned about in letters all the time. I always scratch my head, a bit confused by the question. Oral sex is oral *sex*. It is sex. I do not care what a past president says. It is still being intimate with the private parts of another person. It is not something you would do in public or with just anybody, although the latest statistics of what is happening in this arena with high school students is frightening. Again, you can contract STD's if you choose to go this route. The once-harmless sore throat has taken on threatening ramifications these days as more and more doctors discover young people suffering from venereal diseases in their mouths and throats. This is not a shortcut to having your needs met until you can go all the way. This is just another form of the same exercise. You are not fooling anyone—not God, not yourself, not the man. In the back of his mind he wonders, "Am I the only one who has been treated to such an intimate part of her, or have there been others?" Some things are better saved and kept as pleasant surprises within the confines of marriage. Is oral sex wrong? According to my findings in the Song of Songs in the Bible, the answer is no. But outside of marriage, the answer is a resounding yes.

Now on to the M word. Is masturbation wrong? I have no Scripture verse for you on this one. However, let me bring up a couple of thoughts. What happens after you have cleansed your system of sugar and you happen to have one taste? That's right, it makes you want more. Masturbation lights a fire you will not be able to put out. Temporary relief is replaced with greater longing. Unfulfilled longing can lead to depression, obsession, and oppression which can cause you to reach a breaking point and do something rash. The other part of this equation is you are setting yourself up for difficulty when you do finally get a mate. How can someone please you when you have learned to please yourself? Unless you are highly communicative and demonstrative, he will never be able to duplicate what you have been doing, which could lead to frustration and unfulfillment. Your level of delight and satisfaction would have been easier to reach and maintain minus the self-experimentation.

Again, anytime that we choose to "please ourselves," we are robbing God of worship. He has asked us to present our bodies as a living acrifice, which is in His eyes a reasonable act of worship in exchange for the crucifixion of His Son, who willingly gave up His body and its desire for our sake.

Taking Control

What is a girl to do to handle hormones on the prowl within her body? Redirect your passion, energy, and attention. First, let's deal with your mind. It all starts there. If sex is all you think about, guess what? Your body will follow the cues from your mind. I always cite the story in 2 Samuel chapter 13, of Amnon and Tamar, to give an extreme example of this. Amnon obsesses over his stepsister Tamar, believing himself to be deeply "in love" with her. Actually, he was in "lust" with her. You have to know the difference. If the man in your life is more interested in exploring your body than in investigating your mind, spirit, and personality, get a clue. If the conversations are always superficial, never going to a deeper level, but he is drawing closer to you and pulling on you physically, pay attention. It got to the point where Amnon became sick, he was so overwhelmed with his constant longing for Tamar. It consumed his every thought. When he finally got Tamar in his presence, he raped her. His feelings quickly turned to disgust and hatred. and he basically dumped her! And you thought this only happened in our modern day.

What got him to the point of no return? It was his refusal to get a grip on his thought life. This is difficult in today's culture where we are assaulted with sexual innuendos that permeate everything from a commercial about instant rice, to cars, to the right clothing to wear. Music is so sensual, and if it is not the groove that gets you going, it is the lyrics and their explicit suggestions. What does that mean for you? You must set your own personal boundaries based on your weaknesses. If music gets your thoughts going down the wrong path, then you must become the sentry over your ears and what you allow in. Job, in the book of Job, said he would set no evil thing before his eyes. He knew what he saw fed his mind images that could result in the wrong actions. Avoid movies that tickle your fancy as well as your senses. Conversations could also be added to the list. Talk stimulates our imagination, so reel in your words. Do not start fires you cannot extinguish. We must exercise control over our thoughts and our imagination. Avert your attention to something else that feeds your spirit or gets you stimulated in other ways: a worthwhile project, another area of interest you have been putting on hold. Use all that energy to produce something beneficial for your life and for people around you.

Women laugh when I tell them to find a physical activity in which to get involved. That could be working out, walking, playing tennis, whatever exercise you like to do. A tired body is a satisfied body. The energy in your body has to have an outlet. This is important even if you are married and are free to express yourself sexually. It is amazing to me how many married people are not having sex or are not even interested! It stands to reason that, if this is the case, either the enemy is playing an even more insidious trick on those who should be enjoying their special intimacy with their mates, or sex is highly overrated in the minds of those who have to wait to indulge. Perhaps there is a bit of both going on. But while you are waiting, get in shape so you have a healthy body that you will not be ashamed to present to your marriage partner. Sex can be wonderful when you are healthy, married, and whole in the area of intimacy.

Last, but not least, build up your spirit so it becomes stronger than your flesh. Whatever you feed the most will become the strongest. Center yourself in the Word of God and worship Him. After reading the Bible and having a great time with God before going to bed, your sleep will be sweet and uninterrupted by thoughts of things that you cannot do anything about.

Getting on the Right Track

Why is the area of sexual purity so important for you to master? Because how you deal with this part of your interaction with the man of your dreams will set the course of your relationship and affect your marriage. If you do things God's way in this arena, you will not go to the marriage bed with issues that stop you from enjoying yourself. Premarital sex can stop you from getting to the altar. The perception that a woman has to sleep with a man in order to bind him to her is a deception. In the *New York Times* bestseller *What Men Want* (Avon, 1999), three men who are just regular guys, not trying to be spiritual, confess that men have a double standard when it comes to sex. If you have sex with them too soon, they are disappointed and immediately take you out of the serious-consideration slot and put you in the fun file. If they really care about you, they put off having sex with you to maintain the special nature of the relationship, as well as to keep you in a revered place in their minds. Women usually wonder what is going on when this happens. They wonder if the man is attracted to them. If he is around, he is attracted. He is just trying to respect you. Do not push him to knock you off your pedestal. A man wants to preserve your integrity and image in his eyes if you are the one he feels he might want to marry.

Boaz wanted to preserve the integrity of Ruth privately and publicly. That is what a man will do when he truly loves you and cares about what is

Personal Confession:

I will purpose to guard my heart, as well as my body, and stay focused on the rewards of purity versus its immediate sacrifices.

important to you. The man of your dreams should take just as much responsibility as you do when it comes to maintaining your sexual purity, because it definitely takes two to tango. This can be accomplished by causing him to feel like your high priest. If he feels like the guardian over your spirit and heart, he will rise up and assume the responsibility with honor.

It's All in the Family

Now let's move on to see how Boaz and Ruth's relationship was clinched. I like the next move Boaz made, described in verse 15 of chapter 3. He loaded her down with a large portion of barley, again being cognizant of which needs he could fill in her life immediately. You can also hear the difference in his intent toward her when he says, "Do not go empty-handed to your mother-in-law." He now cares what Naomi thinks because of the relationship he hopes to have with Ruth. The man in your life has to deal with your family. Anything that is precious to you should be precious to him. He should want to make a good impression, as well as a connection with them. If he does not, it is a bad sign. In the end, this type of man will seek to isolate you from your family so he can have "control" over you if he fears too much interference from your family. You have to question his motives when this sort of behavior occurs. The truth of the matter is, you are not just marrying one person. You are marrying into a family.

Some women would like to think they are not marrying the other person's family, but indeed they are. First of all, his father is going to give you big hints on your husband-to-be. This is the man who has been a role model of manhood for him. He will be a lot like his father now, and even more so in the years to come. Because Christ can transform us, your man might be the opposite of his father if there are a lot of things he does not like about his father. You have to be careful to note if your man has released his father and accepted him as he is with love. Or is he bitter? If he is bitter, he can become bound to his father in the spirit and actually end up subconsciously harboring his father's same attitudes and manifesting them in different ways. For example, let's say his father was an alcoholic. He now despises alcohol and the effect alcoholism had on his father because it caused him to be physically abusive to his mother. Now your man does not touch a drop of liquor, but he has an addictive nature. He indulges it in other areas that he does not believe are wrong, and from time to time you feel he can be verbally abusive. It behooves you to observe your man's family and not discard what you see.

Let's talk about family dynamics for a moment. If you are a serious consideration for him, he will want to expose you to his family. If he never introduces you to them, you have not made the serious-consideration list. But if you *do* make it, there is a test you must pass: the mama test. You want a man who loves his mother and treats her well. It is the first indication of how you will be treated. How you get along with his family is important, but let me insert a little warning here. Though it is wonderful to have a great friendship with his mother, be careful. Do not discuss the private things between you and your man with his mother. A man resents it when he feels you are trying to use his mother to get to him. He will exit in a hurry. Try to stay on neutral territory until after the wedding ceremony, and keep his mom out of your courtship. After marriage, have a wonderful friendship with her, but preserve your husband's privacy by not complaining or sharing what goes on between the two of you with the rest of his family.

When it comes to him and your family, observe how he treats them and interacts with them. Is he comfortable with them? How does your family respond to him, especially your father? If a father is not present, then gather information from the other significant male relatives or friends you have. Men know other men and will let you know exactly what type of brother he is without even blinking. They will definitely tell you if he is worthy of your time. Is he kind to your mother and attentive to your siblings? His behavior will let you know just how highly he thinks of you by how important it is for him to make a good impression with your family. If he avoids your family, take note and beware. He might not have the best of intentions toward you. I also suggest not taking him to meet your family until you have met his. It might signal to him you are trying to move the relationship forward before he is ready on your own terms. At the right time, it is important to have people who are more objective than yourself check him out.

We know that Naomi thought highly of Boaz and recommended him to Ruth, so he already had high points. He was well thought of in the community and among his own workers. All the right foundational traits were in place, and then he tops them all off by having special regard not only for Ruth, but also for the only family she had. He sends her away full. The man in your life should add to it, not subtract from you and where you were before he arrived on the scene. He should multiply the fruit in your life, not divide your focus and make you uncertain of the things that once were clear. He should make you full. He should be a man you are not ashamed to present to the world, as well as to your inner circle. He will be an intentional man who makes his plans clear to you so you can walk in confidence.

Man Fact:
A man will do whatever is necessary to be a part of your world once he concludes that is where he wants to be.

He will not leave you to play guessing games. He will furnish you with an answer for all who ask you what is happening in your relationship. Boaz gave her barley and instructions and sent her home.

Boaz said that he would take care of what needed to be done in order to secure Ruth's future. This is a man's job. A real man knows this. When Ruth arrived home, she told Naomi what happened. Then Naomi said something very profound that I think a lot of women overlook: "Sit still, my daughter, until you know how the matter will turn out; for the man will not rest until he has concluded the matter this day" (Ruth 3:18 NKJV). She was right. A man will do what he has to do in order to get what he wants. Listen to what he says and do it. If he asks you to wait and allow him to set some things in order, do it. This is your first test of submission. This is also his test of how he takes the lead and follows through. He has the hard job; your job is easy. All a woman has to do is be ready and wait, not sitting around idly watching time go by, but releasing the matter in her heart and continuing to function. She knows that when everything is in place, the man will "come correct," as we say in Urbanese. Move aside and allow a man to be a man, to exercise his will to make things right for you. Allow him the pleasure of pursuing and winning the prize—you!

Ponder This

- How willing are you to become vulnerable and transparent to a man? What are your fears in this area? What would he need to do to gain your trust?

- Where are you when it comes to maintaining your purity? What are your struggles? What are some working solutions for you?

- Have you reconciled any family issues you have? In what areas do you need healing in order to have more healthy interactions with your loved ones?

Therefore, I urge you, brothers [and sisters] in view of God's mercy, to offer your bodies as living sacrifices, holy and pleasing to God—which is your spiritual worship (Romans 12:1).

10
Where the Rubber Hits the Road

Then Boaz said, "On the day you buy the land from Naomi and from Ruth the Moabitess, you acquire the dead man's widow, in order to maintain the name of the dead with his property." At this, the kinsman-redeemer said, "Then I cannot redeem it because I might endanger my own estate. You redeem it yourself. I cannot do it."

RUTH 4:5-6

Women have no idea what a man has to go through to come to a place of actually embracing the idea and reality of commitment. But once he has made up his mind, it is on! Unbeknownst to Ruth, Boaz had his own little plan to get her hand. He knew exactly how to negotiate this delicate matter. First, he went to find the kinsman-redeemer who really had first rights to marrying Ruth. When Boaz found him, in the presence of witnesses he broached the matter. He informed the relative that Naomi had returned from Moab and sold the property belonging to her husband. It was his option to buy the land back to keep it in the family. Of course, the man wanted the land. He would stand to gain a lot from it. He could plant crops on it, earn back the money used to purchase it in no time, and move on to greater profits. It was not difficult to see what he would get out of the deal. Ah, but when Boaz brought up the fact that Ruth would have to come with the land, the relative changed his tune. He was not interested in adding Ruth to his list of responsibilities. It could cause problems for him and affect his inheritance. No, that was too high a price to pay. He was willing to pass on the land and what he could gain from it in order to avoid having to take care of Ruth.

If a man has no emotional investment in the woman he is seeing, he will always take whatever she is willing to give as long as it does not cost him anything. This is why I always tell women not to give gifts to men right away. After you have been seeing one another for more than six months you can give something small, but keep it to a minimum—nothing personal, nothing large or expensive. Why? Because while he will feel good knowing you thought about him, he does not want to worry about what it all means. *Should I give her something now? Do I have to match it or do better? Does this mean she wants to get serious with me? Gee, I do not know what to do!* It is too much angst for him. A fun card once in a blue moon that makes him laugh is a nice icebreaker with nothing attached to it. Do not overdo it. He does not need a card once a week, just every now and then. Women are givers—we are just wired that way. This is why we need to watch the caregiving in the early stages of a relationship.

In the latter stages of courtship, remain vigilant. We tend to settle in. Resist the urge to behave like a wife until you are one. Leave him wanting more. Stick to pleasant tidbits—little surprises that make him wonder what life would be like with you every day.

Being too available is another area where women become ensnared. We begin to revel in how pleasant the present moment feels and forget about the long-range goal. If a man is comfortable being able to see you whenever he wants, why should he have to think about how to get more of your time? There is an appropriate amount of time to spend with him that allows him to know he is a priority. However, he should never be the only priority. Boundaries should be set to let him know if he wants more of your time, he needs to make a commitment. Or you can have a wonderful time seeing one another almost every day and just play house ad infinitum.

The Value of Love

Have you ever been shopping and seen something you really liked? You think to yourself, *Well, that's been here for a while, so I can come back and get it another time*. Then the salesperson tells you that after this weekend, the item will no longer be available. That information snaps you into making a decision, doesn't it? The idea that the item will no longer be available heightens your urgency to claim it. You knew you liked it, had always admired it, promised to buy it one day, but other things always seemed to be a greater priority. Now it was time to commit to the item or forget about it. The same holds true in relationships. People get comfortable. Next thing you know, couples are dating for six years! Eventually they break up because one of them realizes he or she has been floating endlessly and is tired of the journey. The man meets someone and is married within three months. The ex-girlfriend is shocked! How could this have happened? She was trying to get him to marry her all this time. Her tactic was wrong because she was too available.

When a woman truly knows her value, she does not discount her time or love. She understands it must cost a man something in order for him to appreciate his relationship with her. Think about how you treat things you acquired for free or for a cheap price versus something for which you paid a lot of money. You treat the more expensive possession with great care. You do not leave it lying around just anywhere. You probably even have a special case or place where you store it to keep it from being damaged or broken.

A wise older friend of mine told me once that a man has to see you, pursue you, go through something in order to have you, and win you. These are the four steps a man must master in a significant relationship. Does this mean you should create all kinds of drama in this man's life? Absolutely not. Does this mean you can manipulate him to get what you want? A thousand times, no! What I am saying is, if you had a life before you met this man, you should continue to have one. He should have to win more of your time, as well as your heart. He should respect your time and who you are

Man Fact:
A man will never do more than he has to. This includes making a commitment or anything else you want him to do.

as a woman, while keeping his intentions clear. He will then know that if he wants all of you, he will have to marry you.

Exactly what type of things does a man consider when making that final decision about whether you are the one for him? The first thing, after his feelings for you, is a more practical matter, such as, "Can I take care of her?" This is where your habits might come under some scrutiny. I recall a man telling me about when he went shopping with a woman he was dating. He noticed that as she grabbed the various things she wanted, she never looked at the price tag. This frightened him and eliminated her from further consideration. This man felt she would not be a fiscally responsible wife and could really hurt him financially. A man does consider his future with you. Will he have an inheritance left, or will his bank account be ransacked by impetuous shopping and materialism? Men are afraid of shopaholics. A man wants to know that the woman in his life will be careful in the area of finances.

Your present spending habits will tell him a lot about his future. How are your finances? How do you spend your money? Do you have any savings or investments? Are you always scrambling to pay your bills? Do you live from paycheck to paycheck? How many credit cards do you have? Are they all at their limit? Get it together, my sister. No man wants to inherit debt. The first statement Ruth's next of kin said was he did not want to marry her because it would affect his estate.

The next thing a man checks out is your personal habits. Can he trust you with his heart and his secrets? A woman must master the art of discretion. You may love to talk, but a man gets nervous when you tell your friends too much. He does not like to feel as if he is being discussed all the time. He wants to know the things he shares with you remain with you. You are to be his intimate friend who keeps his secrets and dreams safe.

Another way you let him know if you are able to be trusted with his heart is by how you handle yourself with him. This means you stay pure, which we discussed earlier. However, I want to throw another caveat about this into the mix. When you display self-control with him in the sexual arena, you will win his trust. He will not be worried if he has to leave you for a length of time because he knows you are a woman of principle and integrity who will stand firm in her convictions, even when he is not present.

One more thing in this area of trust. A man does not want to feel that the things he shares with you in the area of weaknesses or mistakes will be thrown back in his face, whether it be at opportune moments when you are upset or when you want something he is not anxious to give. He desires to be accepted, understood, and forgiven. This area of trust is big...don't miss it. The more you replay past conversations with him, the fewer conversations you will have. He will begin to shut down and keep things to himself, to the detriment of your relationship. Relationships thrive when openness is present. When a couple starts withholding information, the gap between them widens. Make your man feel safe to communicate the good, the bad, and the ugly with you without the fear of future repercussions.

Taking Care of You and Yours

When I consider the list of traits that Bathsheba related to her son Solomon about the type of woman he should look for as a life partner in Proverbs 31, not only does she stress how this woman would take care of *him*, but also how she took care of herself and other people. This detailed description was a crystal-clear picture of what her spirit and heart really looked like. You can be on good behavior for only so long before the real you begins to surface in your attitudes toward yourself, as well as toward other people. Ladies, rest assured, you are being watched. Therefore, you have got to have your package together. You see, when Boaz saw Ruth, it was not just her outer beauty that struck him, but her inner beauty as well. There were lots of things about her that were apparent to him and were a major plus.

First, she was resourceful. There is a fine line between being self-sufficient and knowing when to accept help. A man does stop to consider if a woman could handle life if something happened to him and he was not able to be there for her and his family. Would she be a survivor and able to take care of the family? Or would she become a victim, paralyzing her entire family in the midst of their circumstances? No, he wants a woman who can be his partner, helping to carry the load of life between them. He likes a woman who has a plan and a clear vision of where she is going in life and what she would like to have happen. She should be able to laugh at the future because she is prepared for it. She rests in the knowledge that she has certain things in place in her life, and whatever she cannot handle is secure in the hands of God. This sort of security is attractive to a man. It signals to him that life with you will not be one emergency after another. Together, you will be able to implement plans for the future and see them through to fruition.

This brings me to my second point: wisdom. A man wants a woman in his life who brings something to the relationship intellectually. He wants a thinking partner, not a bossy partner, not one who knows everything and is never wrong, not one who always talks and never listens. He wants a thinking woman with grace. He wants someone he can plan his life with and receive wise counsel from during times when he is not quite sure which way to go. He will be watching how you live your life and function in the midst of everyday chaos, how you rationalize situations that may be trying or difficult. Though no man desires a woman who thinks she is smart and will not let anyone forget it, wisdom is important to him.

Even in the course of natural conversation, a typical man is stimulated by a woman who has enlightening things to say. Isn't it interesting that in most cases where a husband runs off with another woman, it is because he finds her to be a more stimulating partner not just sexually, but mentally as well? He feels he has finally met his equal—someone he can really talk to, someone who respects his ideas and thinks he is wonderful. She walks the walk by loving and *serving* him.

Okay, somebody just hyperventilated when she got to the word *serve*. A truly wise woman knows how to make a man feel like a king. She knows that is the quickest route to getting him to treat her like a queen. She pays attention to his needs and makes him feel important in her universe. To a man, this translates as unconditional support, by cheering him on when he does things right and seeking ways to cater to his needs. His need may be as simple as being listened to. A wise woman also knows the power of praise and attentiveness. She listens and understands that what he says is valid and a reality to him, whether she feels it is important or not. She is strong, but soft at the same time, because she has mastered the art of being a woman.

Her strength also lies in her physical health. Do you take care of yourself? Are you fit and healthy, no matter what size? Men generally want a woman who is not going to fall apart on them. They do not know how to handle illness, physical limitations, constant health issues, etc. I am talking about before marriage. If a health crisis occurs after they have committed to you, most will remain with a determination to be there for the woman they love. Before a commitment has been made, a man will think long and hard about volunteering to live with health issues for the rest of his life. I recall after my accident, when I was hit by a car as a pedestrian, my leg was injured quite badly. After my first operation, while I was still in a cast and on crutches, a man who had been pursuing me rather diligently simply disappeared after an evening of watching me struggle with my crutches. A year and a half of therapy and three operations later, another man who had been in my life before and wanted to give it another try decided I was too sedentary for him. He wanted someone who was able to enjoy physical activities with him.

Someone who was in pain and moving slow just was not his cup of tea. However, do not lose hope. These types of situations truly separate the men from the boys!

Every now and then, a rare man steps up to the plate. I recall a very special Christian speaker and singer who suffered a tragic accident and broke her neck. She found herself paralyzed from the shoulders down. She was engaged to a very handsome man at the time. She wondered how her accident would affect their relationship. This wonderful man of God was determined to go the long haul with her. He had his job relocate him to a place where he could be closer to her to assist in her recovery process. He was determined to marry her anyway! She is still in a wheelchair and still paralyzed, though she has gained some movement in her shoulders and arms. They have an eight-year-old son now. When you see how he cares for her, it is enough to make God even more real to you. So you see, there is hope if you are suffering with something physical. God can shape a man's heart around your circumstance. God prepares a special man for a special woman.

Creating an Oasis

How are your homemaking skills? This is another area that has fallen by the wayside in recent years. Men are complaining that women do not cook anymore. In our rush, rush, go, go world, everyone has gotten into the habit of eating out. Small wonder so many women suffer with controlling their weight! All the fast foods and quickie snacks that are loaded with sodium, fat, and sugar were never supposed to be an everyday occurrence. They were the last-ditch option when you could not stop to prepare a fresh meal.

I realize that women, for the most part, do not like to cook because they do not know how. Gone is the era of mothers teaching their daughters how to cook a good meal. I challenge you to find someone who knows how to cook and ask her to show you how to prepare some of the dishes you have tasted and liked. After you have mastered one dish, you will feel more secure to try another and another. Remember, most men have mothers who cook.

And let's not forget how to make a house a home. Many women put off decorating their homes because they do not want to look as if they have settled in before getting married. We have all sorts of excuses for this. *What if he does not like the way I've decorated? I'll have to do it all over again. I'm going to wait until I'm married and then we'll decorate together. It just seems as if I'm giving up on having a partner if I forge ahead with homemaking on my own.* Any of these sound familiar to you? A man wants to know what life would look and feel like with you. One of the ways he judges this is by your home. Make it one he enjoys and gets a sense of warmth from. You can always make it better when the time comes.

Man Fact:
Whether you want to believe it or not, one certain way to a man's heart is still through his stomach!

Recently, I purchased a new home. I have to confess this was the last frontier and a breakthrough for me. I had been holding out, insisting this was the one thing I was going to leave for my future husband to buy for me. After a while, I realized I was not being wise or financially responsible. This was an investment that could reap wonderful returns. Either it would be a home I could sell and have money to contribute to a new home with my husband, or it could become a rental property that adds to our income, or even a second home if I had to move to another state. On that note, I took the plunge and made my purchase without any more hesitation. Therefore, I have been in decorating mode.

When the discussion turned to my bedroom, I decided I wanted a California king-sized bed. Some people wanted to know what a single person was going to do with this huge bed! I explained that the way I sleep, a queen-sized bed is not big enough, I am all over it, plus I do not plan on being alone for the rest of my life. It is kind of the "If you build it, they will come" philosophy from the movie *Field of Dreams*.

Man Fact:
A man envisions what his future with you will look like when he steps into your home. Make it a beautiful picture.

Please take note: It would be my preference that no man moves into my house, but that we acquire another one together. I just believe it helps both people to feel like equal partners. However, not knowing what life will mandate, I am ready either way. Who knows, he might have a bigger, better place! Hopefully, he will let me bring my bed along. In the meantime, I am having a great time making my present house a home—an oasis, a place where people feel good when they visit.

People know when they are in a home versus a temporary holding station. I also believe part of the reason many singles feel as if their life is not complete without a man is because they have done nothing to their environment to give them a sense of completion. When you love the space you live in, you will spend more time rejoicing about the wonderful life you are living and murmuring less about how alone you feel.

Personal Confession:

I will purpose to be a complete package, not just for a man but for myself as well. I will rejoice in all the unique gifts I have as a woman and glorify God by utilizing my talents and abilities to the utmost.

Taking care of business, self, and home, while nurturing a spirit that is a rich reservoir for a man to draw from, puts you in line to be among the chosen. When a man considers what it will cost him to be with you, you must be worth the price. He knows he stands to forfeit his freedom, future plans, finances, and his identity as an autonomous sojourner living life as he chooses. He will have no more of acting on impulse. The sobering thought of replacing spontaneity with sound and responsible game plans can be very overwhelming. He will now be responsible for another human being besides himself, maybe more!

Some men are willing to pay the price, some are not. Based on what you know about your own value and what he perceives your value to be, a decision will be made. As the song goes, "A real man knows a real woman when he sees her." It definitely takes a real man to recognize a woman's worth and be willing to pay the price. Just know that even if you have done all your homework well (be honest with yourself on this one), and that man decides to pass on securing your hand, it is his loss. He simply was not ready. And you do not want a man who is not ready for you.

- In what ways have you cultivated yourself to be a pearl of great price?

- What areas do you need to work on in how you relate to a significant other in your life?

- What things about yourself do you believe to be valuable attributes that a man should desire?

Who can find a virtuous woman? for her price is far above rubies (Proverbs 31:10 KJV).

11

Paying the Cost to Be the Boss

And Boaz said to the elders and all the people, "You are wit-
nesses this day that I have bought all that was Elimelech's,
and all that was Chilion's and Mahlon's, from the hand of
Naomi. Moreover, Ruth the Moabitess, the widow of
Mahlon, I have acquired as my wife."

RUTH 4:8-10 NKJV

This is called stepping up to the plate and doing what has to be done, no matter what the cost. One man considered the cost of marrying Ruth and decided it was too high for him. If he married her and she had sons, they would be entitled to inheriting the land he had purchased in order to gain her hand. This would cost the children he already had because he would be taking money that had been stored up for them to purchase the land from Naomi. He would have to sacrifice one thing in order to gain another with the possibility of no return. There were also concerns about adding another woman to his household. And, last but not least, Ruth was actually a liability because she came adding nothing. She did not have a dowry. Ruth was an expensive woman!

When a man truly loves and wants a woman, no price is too high. He will give his all to acquire his pearl of great price. This is the prototype of a man who earns your love and respect by laying his all on the line. Jesus did it for His collective bride, the church, and He has placed that same spirit in the heart of every real man who understands his position in the love relationship. Consider this fact: Ruth was nowhere around when this transaction or agreement took place. He was quite capable of handling the matter on his own. He did not need Ruth's help figuring out what to do. He knew what he wanted and determined what he had to do to get it.

This is a true test for a woman. It requires patience on her part. When Ruth returned home to Naomi and told her all that had transpired on the threshing floor, Naomi told Ruth to sit and wait. She was not to fret, check on the matter, or try to help Boaz. She told Ruth that Boaz would not rest until he had settled the matter.

Man Fact:
A man will step up to the plate when he is ready to claim you. He will be intentional in the steps he takes to secure your hand in marriage.

Ruth's only job was to relax and let the man take care of business. Oh, if we could only master that one!

Ladies, now is the time to check out the power your man wields in the areas of problem-solving and follow-through. How does he interact with people? How does he handle stress? Is he able to calmly gather the facts, making rational and wise decisions under pressure? Or does he explode, fall apart, or become paralyzed? This is important. Why? Because if you marry this man, you will have to submit to him. Now is *not* the time to ignore warning signs about aligning yourself with a leader whom you will find difficult to follow. Too many woman are so anxious to be married that they do not pay attention to these signs. They are in love; therefore, everything their man does is okay or can be changed later. Noooo! We already had that conversation. What you see is ultimately what you will get. Can you live with him as he is?

There are many traits that need closer inspection. Will you never complain about the way he handles money? His procrastination? Some of his habits? His bad temper? His indecisiveness? His lack of ability to make plans? Do not marry him and then rebel because you have decided he is a fool. This is something you should have known before the wedding. God calls you to honor the commitment you made. I have observed many couples who struggled with their decision and called off the wedding. Then, because of the pressure from peers and family, because the hall had already been paid for, because the invitations had already been sent, they decided to "go through with it." Those words echo in my spirit. The minute anyone says they need to just "go through with it," or "get on with it," or "get it over with," there is trouble. Why no one ever rationalizes that the cost of cancellation *before* a wedding is far less than the cost of a divorce—emotionally as well as financially—*after* the wedding eludes me.

The first spiritual rule of conduct when moving forward with any decision in life is this: When in doubt, do not do it. Take that unsettled feeling as a cue from the Holy Spirit that either this is not the move to make, or it is not the time to make it. Do not move forward unless you have a complete release and peace in your soul about your decision. The only pressure to which you should ever give in is that of the voice of the Lord speaking to your inner woman. You want to be with a man to whom you can wholeheartedly submit.

Healing Past Hurts

Many women who have been accused of being controlling are that way because they want to avoid getting hurt. A woman must deal with her unresolved issues in the area of fear and lack of trust. As a single woman, you should be examining this area of your life and doing the work to heal from past disappointments. If you have ever uttered the words, "I will never allow that to happen to me again," you need to revisit the pain and put it to rest. When we make these types of vows, we set ourselves up for the same situation to revisit us time and time again. We become perpetrators of our own rejection. Because we expect it, we invite it with our defensive attitudes and sabotage a potential relationship with subconscious actions that repel the other person.

Personal Confession:

I will purpose to be patient and wait until I can see the whole picture before making decisions that can affect the rest of my life and the quality of it.

Go back to the hurtful event that is stuck in your spirit. Forgive and release. Settle it in your heart that it was not the fault of the man in your past, that he could not recognize or appreciate what he had in you. God will not allow any relationship to work that is not good for you if you have truly submitted yourself to Him and given Him the free hand to select your mate for you. Learn to cultivate trust in God and not in man. Trust Him to keep you on the right track. Then watch the man who is before you. Relax …wait and allow him to *earn* your trust. Yes, he must earn your trust. How? By keeping his commitment to you. Boaz told Ruth he would take care of the mat-ter, and he did. He was what we call an intentional man. This type of man is what we are all looking for.

Personal Confession:

I will remain open and transparent in my relationship, as well as accountable to those who are in authority over me. I will receive and weigh their counsel carefully before moving forward according to my feelings.

The Nature of a Man

Now, I must caution you here on the pattern of men. First, there is the Fast Talker. His pattern is easy to chart. He comes on strong from the beginning. He overwhelms you with atten-tion and seems to know all the right things to say…the cute things to do. He knows you are the one and has your head spin-ning. This is like the movies. Everything is happening so fast. It is just the way you imagined it would be in your dreams. It is so romantic! It is almost too good to be true. You are right. It *is* too good to be true. This man starts off fabulous, but finishes badly. He runs out of steam just as quickly as he began. He usually has no good explanation for ending the relationship, so he merely disappears in a puff of smoke, leaving you shattered and bewil-dered. After all, you thought he really cared for you and you trusted him.

When this man appears on the scene, you have two options. One, you can recognize him for what he is and not invest your heart. This man can usually only maintain his level of pursuit for one to three months before dissolving in a heap of exhaustion. His usual record is about a month if he lives in the same city with you. If it is a long-distance relationship, it could continue for several months simply because he has the relief of no physical accountability. He could actually be juggling several relationships without you even knowing it. This type of man knows all he has to do is call all of his women once a day to let them know he is thinking of them. For most women, this is enough because we are moved by what we hear. As long as our ears are tickled, nothing else is required. Always remember: Actions speak louder than words. If you are only hearing from him but not seeing him, this is a bad sign. If he wants to suck up all of your time immediately, this, too, is a bad sign. No one can keep going at this pace without imploding. Trust will always be an issue with this guy. Consider this: He is smooth because he has had a lot of practice. Don't be a stand-in.

The other option you have with the Fast Talker, if you truly think he has potential in spite of himself, is to force him to slow down his pace. You will be doing both of you a favor. It will free both of you to see one another as you truly are and allow you to make realistic decisions concerning how, and if, you want to proceed with the relationship. It will give you the opportunity to keep your head clear and make a discerning evaluation of this man's character—if he should go in the friendship file or the potential-mate file. Every woman should have a file. Do not throw anyone out unless he is detrimental to your mental and spiritual health. Otherwise, file according to his actions.

The next is the Drifter. This man does not know what he wants. All he knows is that he enjoys being with you. He has no steady pattern, which keeps you off balance because you have no idea where you stand with him. He does not really make plans with you because he never knows what he will feel like doing. He makes you feel like an afterthought. He checks in with you just enough to keep you on his string. He is nice enough, and you do have a good time when you finally get together, so you decide to ride it out, investing your trust and emotions, though you have no sure indication where you will end up with this person. Waiting on this man is not wise. He needs a gentle confrontation. It is as simple as asking him one question: "You know, we have been seeing each other for a while, and I really enjoy talking with you and being with you, but I am unsure of exactly what is happening between us. Where do you see our relationship going?" If he says he had not given it any thought or he does not know, it is time to be assertive for your own sake. So, here is your next line: "Thank you for being honest with me. I also have to be honest with you. I can't continue to see you because my feelings are becoming involved. If you have no intentions of pursuing a committed relationship, I feel the need to protect my heart and move on." At this point, he will either retreat to give it some thought and come back with a definite answer on how he would like the relationship to proceed, or he will release you. Of course, he might still check in for a while to see if he can maintain a "friendship" with you. But it would only be for his own convenience and not for your benefit at all. I suggest you be unavailable for further drifting toward a place called nowhere.

Do not be afraid to confront the Drifter. It is the only way you will be able to know what course you are on. All Drifters are not bad. Some simply drift because they do not feel the need or urgency to chart a course. They assume everything is cool just the way it is, and they will not make a decision until they have to.

Some Drifters, on the other hand, are commitment phobes. They drift because they can. They enjoy the benefits of having a relationship without the commitment for as long as they can. When questioned, they move on. A woman must never seek to control a man. But she can control her own course by the decisions she makes. She can choose to be in an aimless relationship and emerge from the experience hurt and disillusioned years later. Or she can take her life back and decide she wants a more sure existence where she is aware of exactly where she is heading. We are all too mature for relying on daisies to let us know if "he loves me, he loves me not."

And last, but certainly not least, is the Slow but Steady man. I believe that Boaz fell into this category. He watched Ruth from afar. He made provision for her, made sure she was safe, but he did not make any other moves. Remember, she was in his field for approximately two to three months. The Slow and Steady male is like the turtle in the race between the tortoise and the hare. He may not move quickly, but he does finish the race. Most of the time, Mr. Slow but Steady knows what he wants but sets his course, works on getting all his ducks in a row, and then waits to confirm he is making the right choice. He takes his time checking out how consistent you are. Are you the woman he really thinks you are? As soon as that is settled in his heart, he declares what he wants and moves forward with plans to secure your hand in marriage. Now this man might be the least exciting out of the group, but he is the one who will give you the most secure future. He will also surprise you with a peace and joy you have never known before because he is a man you can trust to hold your heart.

This is the man some women pass on because they want more spice in their lives. He is not their "type," so to speak. However, let's examine what your type really is. In this context, has a relationship with your type of man ever worked out? What does that say about your type? Some of us have broken choosers. We like a certain type of man, but that man is not good for us. Let's face it. There is something very appealing about the "bad boy," the "rebel," and the "ladies' man." Ever since the silver screen graced us with intoxicating images of men like James Dean, Elvis, and James Bond, up to present-day guys like Johnny Depp, Denzel Washington, and Superman, we have been holding out until our fantasies can become reality. It does not happen. Real relationships require real men.

Good men are really not that hard to find. The truth of the matter is most women don't realize that good men are *made* by consistant communication, respectful boundaries, and loving acceptance of who he is as a man.

Decent guys have a hard time capturing our attention because they might not have rehearsed all the silky lines that make us swoon, or mastered the art of wearing the right clothing or shoes, or learned to be as spontaneous and creative as we would like them to be in their pursuit of us. But these men are solid, real men, with real passions and with lots of love to give. A good man is a slow and steady man who means what he says and follows up his words with action as proof of his sincerity, integrity, and love for you.

The Slow but Steady man is not interested in keeping his relationship with you on the "down low," as the saying goes. He is not for romance under wraps. He wants the world to know, or those who matter to him, anyway, about the good thing he has found. He is open and intentional in his relationship with you and will not reduce your relationship to guessing games. Now, ladies, understand that a man is often not a massive talker. He will probably assume you understand his intentions by his actions. A man does not do things just to do them. He is very deliberate about what he says and does. When Boaz made that move to redeem the hand of Ruth, he made sure he had witnesses. The man was serious, okay? He left nothing to chance. He secured the deal with his next of kin to marry Ruth and then made sure it was seen by other people.

In Ghana, West Africa, I love the tradition of the engagement before the wedding. It is a very serious matter. The groom has to make an appointment with the family of the bride to come and ask for her hand. It is referred to as "the knocking."

Personal Confession:

I will be open to the possibility of dating men who are not my type. I vow not to write off potential mates because they do not fit my preconceived notions. I will allow God to steer my course in all my relationships.

I'm giving you the modernized version of this, as it was an even more involved series of events in the past. On the appropriate day, the groom, along with significant members of his family, goes to the family home of the bride bearing gifts, and formally asks for her hand. If it is granted, they proceed to make a day when "the engagement" will be made official. The day of the engagement can be as intricately planned as the wedding itself. Both sets of family gather. The older members of the family usually officiate the engagement. They tell stories and exchange banter about the two who have decided to marry. They give instruction to the couple on how to care for one another. The groom presents gifts to the family and asks formal permission from her immediate family to marry her. The father, mother, brothers, everyone must agree. He then presents the ring to her, and a major celebration with food and drink seals the engagement. It is a public declaration of their intent to become husband and wife.

Their word on that day is taken so seriously that they are considered married, even though the wedding ceremony has not taken place. In order to break the engagement, another family meeting would have to be held. The entire family would be involved, and they would be held accountable to the elders for their decision. It would not be easy to get out of the engagement. They would be urged to work out their differences before permission to go their separate ways would be granted.

It would serve us well in this country to imitate this practice. The solemnity of the promises you make to one another is fully realized. But even better is the covering it provides for a woman. How can you apply this tradition to your situation? Get the blessing. I believe it does a man good to have to ask a woman's family for permission to marry her. It keeps him rooted in the reality that what he is about to do is serious, and he will be held accountable by someone other than you. It is important for both of you to get your family's blessing. This step is crucial.

> **Man Fact:**
> A man with pure motives will want the blessing of your inner circle on your relationship. He will not be afraid to be held accountable to them because his intentions toward you are honorable.

Parental Blessing

After Boaz made his intentions clear before the elders at the gate, they not only witnessed the transaction between Boaz and his kinsman in regard to Ruth, they also declared a blessing over

Boaz and his future wife. For every woman or man I have ministered to who has been on the verge of divorce or is divorced, the same words have been repeated when I asked them how their parents felt about their spouse. "Oh, they did not like him. They did not want me to marry him." The parents might have gone along with the wedding plans to keep the peace, but they most certainly did not give their blessing. The absence of that blessing might as well have been a curse. It usually foretells of problems to come.

I think of the story of Samson found in Judges chapter 14. He goes off and selects his own bride, completely shirking the tradition of the bridegroom's father selecting a bride for his son. Samson then boldly, against his parents' wishes, pushed them to make all the arrangements for the wedding and accept his choice. Well, the rest is history. Shortly after the marriage, his bride betrayed him, and he went off in a murderous rage, making quite a few enemies. Shortly after he calmed down, he went to retrieve his bride from her father's house, only to find out she had been given to his best man! Well, he cannot say his parents did not warn him, that is for sure. I am certain they did not foresee all the turmoil. All they knew was they did not feel this woman was the right one for him. Call it a parent sense or third sense if you will, but I believe that God gives parents a special sensitivity to the needs of their children, whether the parents are believers or not.

I think back to my own college sweetheart whom both of my fathers, Mr. McKinney and Mr. Hammond, resoundingly, hands down, voted out of my life. Oh, how I cried and railed. I was caught up in a modern-day Romeo and Juliet story! Every time I went through another failed relationship, I would think back to my old flame who loved the ground I walked on and say to myself that I could have been married by now if it was not for my fathers. And, of course, my mother had joined in with them.

Well, I can tell you now that they were absolutely right. At an age where I could not see the character of my beloved, my fathers could. Today that man I wanted to marry so badly is in jail for murdering a man. He beat him to death in a rage. That is who I would have been married to!

Whether you like it or not, parents have radar on these sorts of things. Their eyes are not glazed over with a delicate shade of rose as they look over at your potential mate. Because they love you and know you, they are able to make dis-

Man Fact:
Men know one another. Always have a man or another brother in your life check out your potential love. They will give you the real scoop, no holds barred!

cerning and objective observances of the person you present to them. Embrace the idea that God has placed parents in our lives to keep us safe—in some instances, to save us from ourselves and our sometimes impetuous, foolish choices.

You might feel that you are an adult, you are grown, and you have been on your own for a long time; therefore, your parents should not have any say-so over your life. The Scripture verse that urges us to honor our father and our mother, with the promise that if we do we will have a long life and good success, rings true and has been proven so. Honoring includes considering their words, not just being nice to them. Honor has to do with obedience. No matter what age you are, they are still your parents and have the right to speak into your life. No matter how you feel, I urge you to be careful. Do not go down the aisle without that blessing! This is the greatest gift a parent can give you on your wedding day because God will honor the prayers and words of your parents.

Let me interject here that God honors the words and prayers of parents who honor their children. God answers prayers and heeds confessions He agrees with, not those spoken with a mean spirit or evil motive. I sadly realize that not everyone has had a picture-perfect family life. Some people have been abused emotionally and physically by their fathers and mothers. In this case, your parents might not be the ones to give you the blessing. Seek it from someone grounded in wisdom whom God can use as a spiritual parent to you. It might be your pastor or a godly couple in your life.

I cannot stress enough how important it is to submit your intentions to a group of people you love and trust, and really absorb their counsel. This is your safety net. If you are hesitant about this, that should let you know there is something you do not want to hear. Heed the Word of God and the words of those He has placed in your life to counsel you. It literally could be a matter of life and death—the life or death of your joy, peace, and every romantic dream you ever had of your future. Take the time for marriage counseling and get a release from your pastor and your own spirit to proceed. If you do your homework before the wedding, your marriage will have a greater chance of being fruitful, joyful, and victorious.

As mature and self-made as Boaz was, even he needed the blessing and accepted it graciously. He saw it as a covering that would keep his relationship with Ruth safe. On the wings of that blessing, he moved forward to secure her hand in marriage, and we are still hearing about this incredible love story today. With the blessing in place, your marriage becomes fertile ground for bearing fruit that will serve as a testimony to other people of the faithfulness of God. In a world where people cry out to see good examples of marriage that renew their faith in true love, you can be a blessing and a beacon to those you know and love.

- Consider the man who is your potential mate. What characteristics about him do you treasure most?

- What concerns you about him and your relationship? How can these habits affect your marriage?

- If not presently dating, how open are you to considering someone who is not your type? How has your mindset hindered you from finding true happiness?

- What people in your life would you consider important enough to get a blessing from?

Where no counsel is, the people fall: but in the multitude of counselors there is safety (Proverbs 11:14 KJV).

12
The End of the Matter

So Boaz took Ruth and she became his wife; and when
he went in to her, the LORD gave her conception,
and she bore a son.

RUTH 4:13 NKJV

What a beautiful picture of completion Boaz and Ruth paint with their happy ending. Here is a couple who did it the right way. There is something to be said for that. What starts off right, in most cases, finishes right. What starts off wrong, well…usually never gets right. It just gets worse. Not that I want to mess up a good love story, but I do not want you to just be married. I want you to be married to reality as well. Just because they did everything right at the start of the marriage does not mean that every day was bliss. I am sure they had lots of adjustments to make. Boaz had been single for quite a while. Ruth had been married before and had her own way of doing things. Both of them had to work toward becoming one, as any couple does.

I want you to be equipped to stay on your journey, even after you have finally been found by your Boaz. There are a few things that you need to consider before you start jumping up and down because you finally "caught the fish." Once you catch a fish, that is when the real work begins. You have to clean it and prepare it to be edible. The same goes for marriage. However, most people are so busy gazing through rose-colored lenses that they are shocked when the real work begins. This would be the work of clearing your mind of preconceived notions of what your marriage is *supposed* to look like. You are no longer single. Now the journey begins of becoming one. Both of you will be bringing ideas and habits to the marriage that the other person did not expect. This is where things can go wrong quickly if you do not have some foundational plans under your belt.

In today's world of prenuptial agreements and no-fault divorce, the true meaning of marriage has been lost. It has been reduced to a "well, let's see if this works" format—a loveless contract. Whatever happened to those famous words that Ruth uttered to her mother-in-law, that I am sure she repeated to her new husband, Boaz? "Don't urge me to leave you....Where you go I will go....Your people will be my people and your God my God" (Ruth 1:16). Ruth understood the meaning of covenant, and so did Boaz.

You see, contracts can be broken. Every contract comes laden with loopholes. It is to protect the interest of the person who is making the agreement in case the other party does not live up to the standards of the contract. It is usually for a specified term and has agreed-upon requirements. If any of the specifics are not carried out, the deal is off because the interest of one person was not met. A lot of marriages are like that. Two people stand at the altar in the presence of witnesses and promise to love one another for richer, for poorer, in sickness and in health, 'til death parts them, but then promptly forget their promise the first time a major trial hits. They both retreat to their own corner to ponder which of their needs are not being met by the other partner. Accusations fly. They come to the conclusion they have irreconcilable differences, and the contract is broken. Herein lies the problem. Marriage is not a contract. It is a covenant.

The Power of Covenant

A covenant is different from a contract. There are no specified terms or expiration dates. It is forever and ever, amen. When God made a covenant with Abraham, He sealed it by appearing to him as a flaming torch passing between the split carcass of a dead animal. This was to signify the covenant was sealed in blood. This meant that one of them would have to die in order for the covenant to no longer be in effect. In the mind of God, even death does not alter a covenant. He made a covenant with David, king of Israel, that the throne would never be taken from his family lineage. Even though David messed up badly and eventually died, God honored the covenant by continuing to place David's descendants on the throne right down to Jesus Himself!

When we make a covenant at the altar by saying the profound words "'til death do us part," God expects us to honor our vow. Otherwise, we destroy everything that we have worked for. According to His Word, "As iron sharpens iron, a friend sharpens a friend" (Proverbs 27:17 NLT). This has to be true of the marriage covenant. Two people come together in order to become one. Perhaps this is where the ball

Personal Confession:

I will choose to honor the commitment I made before God and my mate. I will work through issues until a place of compromise and agreement can be made and embrace these adjustments that will take me to the next level of victorious living.

gets dropped. Because we do not have a true understanding of a covenant and the purpose of marriage, we balk at the first sign of a part of ourselves dying. But something has to die in each partner in order for them to become one. We must agree to lay down individual rights in order to grasp the greater good. Oneness empowers us to get further in life than we would individually.

I Did It My Way

Recently, I was on a radio interview discussing my book *In Search of the Proverbs 31 Man* (WaterBrook, 2003). A listener called in and was still disturbed by the guests before me who had written a book called *The Best Thing I Ever Did for My Marriage*. The premise of their book (from what I was able to glean from the interviewer and caller) was what a woman could do for her man in order to make their marriage better. The caller was upset because she felt the authors were saying that all the work in the relationship was on the woman. She wanted to know, "What about the men? Don't they have to do anything?" She then went on into deeper, more dangerous waters by saying that in today's *new* Christianity, people should be able to be independent in a marriage and still get along!

My first reaction was that I did not know there *was* a new Christianity. I had not gotten the memo. No one had informed me that God had changed His mind on anything He had written, or changed His Word in any way. I cited that God is the same yesterday, today, and forever. Therefore, His rules on marriage have not changed. The bottom line is that *both* people, man and woman, are called to submit to one another. The man's assignment is clear: to protect, provide for, love, and cherish his woman. The woman is still called to submit to, respect, and serve her husband. This is something she will do naturally if the man is doing his job.

If he is *not* doing his job, she should continue doing the right thing anyway. Two wrongs do not make a right. Her lifestyle, not her demands, will make a change in him because God will honor her for staying in the right place. I know that might sound too simple, and sometimes the condition of a marriage is far more complicated. However, no one should cause you to sin. We are called to do all that we do as unto the Lord, knowing in the end that is who we will answer to. If that man does not behave, God will deal with him in His own way. God is serious about men treating women properly. I think that most women do not realize this. God will actually stop honoring his progress!

A covenant says you keep your end of the bargain no matter what. God kept His end of the deal with David in spite of his failings. Keep in mind that David was not exempt from suffering the consequences of his actions. Again, I am not encouraging a woman to remain in an abusive marriage that may be hazardous to her health, mentally or physically, or dangerous to the well-being of her children. What I am saying is that, for the most part, we have cultivated an independent society that grows more selfish by the decade. *What about what I want? What about what I need?* This attitude cannot be carried into a covenant relationship. A covenant relationship is based on give-and-take, on dying and dying again, until all that stands between the two of you has passed away. It is no longer *I*, but *we*. I can always tell where a relationship stands between two people by the language they use. I can tell which partner is having a struggle, not just by body language—who leans in and who leans away—but also by their words. One will say, "*We* are going to do this." The other will say, "*I* am going to do this."

When we come into covenant with God, we are called to die daily, to take up our cross and walk, to sacrifice the urgency of our flesh for the call of the Spirit. The closer we draw to God while laying aside anything that stands in the way of our relationship with Him, the more blessed we become. We become more free to experience the life we want after all—filled with righteousness, peace, and joy in the Holy Ghost. The peace that passes all understanding fills us to overflowing because we have finally gotten ourselves out of the way. The same is true in our physical relationships.

How is this achieved? It is done by getting the focus off ourselves and truly seeking to know the other person. What are his needs, his desires, the things that move his heart and make him feel loved and secure? We will discover our own needs being met as we pour out our lives to that other person. The natural response for the other person is to give back because there is no room for him to consider what he lacks. A breakdown happens when your husband tries to fill the needs he feels you are ignoring. Do not give him the room to go there. When he is satisfied, he will seek to satisfy you. This applies to every level of the relationship: from conversation, to daily interaction, to the intimacy of the marriage bed.

Personal Confession:

I will "get over myself" and choose to put my mate first, knowing that God will honor my submission and sacrifice with great rewards— emotionally, as well as in my marriage.

The story tells us that Boaz took Ruth to be his wife. In the King James version it says that Boaz "knew" her, and she conceived and bore a son. As a couple takes the time to truly know one another and unselfishly fill one another's needs, their marriage will bear fruit in accordance with God's timing and design.

Whether that be in the form of children or spiritual fruit, God chooses what will glorify Him most in the life of each couple. Most importantly, their love will continue to grow because it is being nurtured and fertilized with acts of kindness and self-lessness.

As I look at couples who have been together for a long time, who have weathered the storms and worked through their differences, I get a picture of what God had in mind: oneness. They even begin to look alike. They anticipate one another's needs and finish one another's sentences. I see tender men and women who are in tune with one another. When commenting on this to these couples, they are quick to say it was not always that way. They had their struggles, but they endured.

In order to find common ground with our mates, we must be willing to move ourselves out of the way and truly hear the other person. Our love for each other should compel us to seek the other's greater good. Two people inclined toward this end bring out the best in one another and bear fruit that feeds not only them, but also people around them. It restores the faith of singles who have lost hope in the idea of marriage. It makes children feel safe when they look at their parents and see nothing but love and cooperation. This feeling of safety makes children better members of society, whole and balanced. They are able to go out into the world and have meaningful relationships, mirroring what they see at home.

The Truth About Your House

There is a prevalent attitude in our society that says, "It is nobody's business what goes on in my house." This philosophy cannot be further from the truth. What happens in your house will eventually affect other people. A divided house affects everyone in the house. When people leave the house, their attitudes can seriously affect others, sometimes to deadly proportions.

God meant for a covenant to give people security and strength to go out into the world and perform at their best. They are to be infused by the love they get at home and have it be contagious at school, in the marketplace, wherever they go.

The entire concept of two people becoming one has far-reaching implications. Your oneness becomes a legacy that is left to the next generation. Two people having a relationship steeped in wholeness produces children who go on to affect society long after you have departed the earth. Ruth and Boaz had a son, who had a son, who had a son that changed the entire destiny of a nation. Not only that, but their descendant was of the lineage of Jesus Christ. The fruit we bear in our homes eventually affects the world at large, whether we will ever witness the effect or not. What type of fruit do you bear in your home?

The Fruit We Bear

I find it ironic that Ruth (meaning "friendship") had no children by her first husband—you know, the one named Mahlon (his name meant "sickly"). Nothing can grow in a sickly environment and become whole. Because Mahlon was sickly, their marriage bore no fruit except death. Though we all can be transformed by the power of the Spirit of God, some people never experience the breakthroughs they could because of their state of mind. Mahlon was probably used to being sickly and had accepted his fate, no longer seeking a solution or victory for his life. Attitude is everything when dealing with the issues of life. With a sickly frame of mind, he would not have the strength to rise above where he was in order to give birth to something different in his life.

This is why it is so important for a woman to truly know and be cognizant of the character of a man before she marries him. Boaz (meaning "strength") was made of the right stuff. He had what was required for bearing rich fruit. A woman is called not only to be a helper for her husband, but also to be his friend. This is one of the greatest needs a man has from the woman in his life. That man is not called just to be a provider and protector for the woman. He was designed to be her strength. These two characteristics cement them as a couple.

When friendship is joined to strength, incredible things happen. A couple has the ability to give birth to things that will leave a rich legacy—a testimony of a marriage that is a fine example for other people to aspire to and follow. Children with a heritage of sound character and integrity can make wonderful contributions to the people around them and perhaps even to the world.

And how about your own personal satisfaction? When you lay your head down at the end of the day and look at your husband, your Boaz, lying beside you, your heart swells with joy. Through tears of gratefulness to God, you are able to say quietly in your heart: *This man was well worth the wait.*

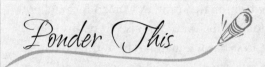

Ponder This

- What is your understanding of a covenant?

- Why do you want to be married? What do you expect to get out of it? What are you prepared to give and leave behind?

- What lasting legacy would you like your marriage to have?

For this reason a man will leave his father and mother and be united to his wife, and they will become one flesh (Genesis 2:24).

Other Books by
Michelle McKinney Hammond

What to Do Until Love Finds You
Secrets of an Irresistible Woman
Where Are You, God?
Get a Love Life
If Men Are Like Buses, Then How Do I Catch One?
Prayer Guide for the Brokenhearted
What Becomes of the Brokenhearted?
How to Be Blessed and Highly Favored
Get Over It and On With It
Why Do I Say "Yes" When I Need to Say "No"?
Sassy, Single, & Satisfied
The Unspoken Rules of Love
In Search of the Proverbs 31 Man
101 Ways to Get and Keep His Attention
The D.I.V.A. Principle
The D.I.V.A. Principle: A Sistergirl's Guide
The Power of Being a Woman
Finding Ms. Right

To correspond with Michelle McKinney Hammond,
you may write to her:
c/o Heartwing Ministries
P.O. Box 11052
Chicago, IL 60611
E-mail her at heartwingmin@yahoo.com
Or log on to her website at:
www.michellehammond.com
or www.heartwing.org

For information on booking her for a
speaking engagement:
Call 1-866-391-0955 or log on to
www.michellehammond.com